GESTURE OF AWARENESS

GESTURE
OF
AWARENESS

A Radical Approach to Time, Space, and Movement

Charles Genoud

WISDOM PUBLICATIONS • BOSTON

Wisdom Publications
199 Elm Street
Somerville, MA 02144 USA
www.wisdompubs.org

Library of Congress Cataloging-in-Publication Data
Genoud, Charles.
  Gesture of awareness : a radical approach to time, space, and move-
ment / Charles Genoud.
    p. cm.
  ISBN 0-86171-506-3 (pbk. : alk. paper)
  1. Spiritual life—Buddhism. I. Title.
  BQ5660.G46 2007
  294.3'444—dc22

                                        2006028464

ISBN 0-86171-506-3

First Printing
10 09 08 07 06
5 4 3 2 1

Cover design by Rick Snizik. Interior design by Gopa&Ted2, Inc. Set in Columbus MT 11/14 pt.
Excerpt from *Tracing Back the Radiance* by R.E. Buswell reprinted with permission. Copyright 1992 by University of Hawaii Press.

Wisdom Publications' books are printed on acid-free paper and meet the guidelines for permanence and durability set by the Committee on Production Guidelines for Book Longevity of the Council on Library Resources.

Printed in the United States of America

CONTENTS

It is over.

But how can it be over before anything has started? And can anything really start? To start something implies that it will go on, will end. That is the movement of time. But is there truth in this sense of movement? To start something is to step into time, and to step into time is to step out from reality into an insubstantial world of images, of language. Therefore, to start, to go on, to be over—may all be equally illusory.

> *Strictly speaking, time does not exist, yet we have to submit to it. Such is our condition. Whether it is a question of passively borne duration—physical pain, waiting, regret, remorse, fear—or of organized time—order, method, necessity—in both cases, that to which we are subjected does not exist. But our submission exists. We are really bound by unreal chains. Time, which is unreal, casts over all things, including us, a veil of unreality.*[1]

Say what one will, something has begun.

Fifteen years ago I discovered a practice called sensory awareness at a workshop led by Michael Topphof, a Dutch psychotherapist. Participants were asked to walk, sit, or lie down. Sometimes we were asked to work in groups of two or three, placing our hands on the shoulders or feet or some other part of the body of another person. We were asked to take the arm of another and to move it slowly.

It was a simple, powerful practice, and such interactions found immediate reflection in the quality of my attention. Straight away I was fascinated by the work, by its power to bring forth life in present experience. By its power to allow present experience to shine. By that time, I had practiced meditation in the Tibetan and Theravada traditions for over ten years. The impact of sensory awareness in my meditation practice was profound. It helped me to be grounded, more balanced. And I loved the playfulness of it.

After the first workshop, I decided to learn more about sensory awareness, and to use it as a stepping stone for the practice of meditation. I attended more workshops with Topphof in Spain, France, and Switzerland and I attended workshops in Mexico with Charlotte Sealver, the pioneer in the field of sensory awareness. All the while I continued with my studies and practice of Tibetan and Theravada Buddhism. When I started to lead Gesture of Awareness classes, I didn't know whether it would only help introduce people to meditation or if it would also lead to insight and wisdom.

Gesture of Awareness is simply a name, one I have given to a meditation of inquiry and mindfulness. It is based mainly on awareness through sensations of the body, and yet it does not imply observation of movement or position. Gesture of Awareness is rather an invitation to experience oneness of body and mind. It is an invitation to experience the body as a body of presence. Experience not through concentration, but through awareness manifesting as a Gesture. Awareness, manifesting as hearing, seeing, thinking, tasting and touching and smelling. But awareness can be veiled by thoughts.

Through the years, through every retreat I led, I would discover new ways of disclosing the many preconceptions that shape and restrain our lives. The preconceptions that lead us to be taken in by the fiction of time and space, here and now. The preconceptions that lead us, for example, to perceive the world through the notion of efficiency.

The practice we engage in during Gesture of Awareness retreats is an inquiry into the nature of such fictions. It questions the chains of time in all their myriad forms: the chains of transformation, improvement, usefulness, and of movement. Questioning, and yet not looking for conclusion, for knowledge, as that would reduce one's experience to the concept of experience.

After studying Buddhism for a few years in India I began to think that such a system of inquiry was the only and correct system. And this worried me. I realized then that it was important for me to not be drawn in by such a narrow way of viewing the spiritual path. It was important to remain open to the possibility that other traditions could also be perfectly true.

If truth is ineffable, ungraspable—as all spiritual traditions acknowledge it to be—how can some have it and claim that others do not? And if such is possible, doesn't that mean truth itself is but a thing and not in itself the truth?

One may need generosity to approach the truth. One needs humility in order to practice generosity. Humility may be learned through begging—to really know how to give one may have to learn how to ask, to beg.

In a similar way, in order to teach one may need to learn just how to learn from others outside one's own system. Discovering in the beliefs and points of view of others that which may bring light to one's own way of seeing and expressing the world.

After returning to the West from India in 1973, I decided along with my friend Fred von Allmen to go to France for a few days of solitary retreat at Hautecombe Abbey, a Catholic retreat center beside Bourget Lake. We were left to ourselves. We weren't even asked to provide any assistance to the monastery. There was a monk, though, whose daily task was to meet with the guests of the monastery. One day, I thought it would be more gracious if I at least joined him for a walk, and while we were together I took the opportunity of asking him if I would be saved, since I didn't believe in God. He asked me what I did believe in, and I said that the ultimate nature of the world was emptiness. The monk replied that no one could say that this belief was not a belief in God. And through this reply the monk showed more tolerance, more openness, than I did.

Years later, engaged in research for my book, *La Non-Histoire d'une Illusion* (The Non-Story of an Illusion), I began to read the work of Christian mystics, most especially that of the thirteenth-century Meister Eckhart. The source of the monk's answer dawned. I discovered Meister Eckhart's clarity: he doesn't give anything that one could grasp as being God. He uses striking expressions, such as "to pray to God to free oneself from God." Meister Eckhart's emphasis on non-grasping is powerfully conveyed in his sermon on poverty, "Bless the Poor in Spirit." A poor man or woman, he says, is a person who wants nothing, has nothing, and knows nothing. If a person has nothing, and yet still has some place within where God can know himself, then he or she is not truly poor. The skill of this mystic at not providing anything at all to grasp is remarkable.

Burned at the stake for heresy in 1310, Marguerite Porete, the French Beguine, is also richly provocative. She wrote of the absence of will. One should practice meditation, she said, without aim, without reason, without any *why*.

I first encountered this notion, though, in *Inner Experience,* a work by the modern novelist Georges Bataille. Any spiritual practice done for future benefit, he said, subjects itself to this benefit, and is therefore completely conditioned. He vehemently negates any possibility of salvation or freedom that would thereby be attained. Attainment and true freedom are as irreconcilable as a crow and an owl, as Tibetan debating students learn. Where one is, the other is not. In his *Theory of Religion,* Bataille investigates not only the relationship between a tool and its user, but so too the relationship between sacrifice and purpose. Such notions bring to light the correspondence between intentional practice and the impossibility of freedom.

Bataille looks at the world from an uncommon angle. During the *intifada* in Israel, for example, a French magazine published a photograph showing boys throwing stones at Israeli soldiers. But one photographer went behind the boys and caught not only the boys but so too the wall of photographers facing them. There were about twenty photographers and five boys. Bataille is fond of questioning the way we may frame our vision of ourselves. He is concerned with wasting, not with accumulating; he is concerned with uselessness, not with efficiency.

Turning one's attention from world to subject may be quite disturbing. The unreality of self is a challenging notion for anyone studying Buddhism. It is difficult to even imagine the possibility of nonexistence. It seems to me that one way of coming to understand the very artificiality of the self is through the study of the way self is created in childhood—the way separation is made between subject and an objective world.

At the Mont Pèlerin Tibetan Center for Buddhist Studies, Geshe Rabten taught philosophy and epistemology. He had a great talent for making readily clear even subtle aspects of Buddhist doctrine. He had a special skill in finding enlightening examples. I found his teachings precise, interesting, and yet something was lacking for me, and this was because there was no notion of a diachronic approach to epistemology. There was no explanation as to how separation of the world into self and perceived world is created in a child's mind. But study of the matter could help one to understand the possibility of an experience free of any such dichotomy. If the world can be separated into subject and object—if the world can be constructed—it is artificial. If it is artificial, it can be deconstructed.

Wandering one day in a bookstore in Geneva, a book called *The Child's Conception of the World* by Jean Piaget caught my attention. I began to read it with great interest, and found that it addressed what had been missing for me from the Buddhist approach to epistemology. Piaget raised questions that specifically concerned this investigation of how a child comes to learn herself in the world:

> *In estimating the child's conception of the world the first question, obviously, is to decide whether external reality is as external and objective for the child as it is for us. In other words, can the child distinguish the self from the external world?*[2]

Piaget later addresses this complex question:

> *Mach showed that the distinction between the internal or psychic world and the external or physical world is far from innate. It arises from action, which, engendered in a reality, of itself undifferentiated, comes little by little to group images about one or the other of these two poles, round which two intercorresponding systems are built up.*[3]

Mystics, philosophers, and psychologists have not been idle these past 2,500 years since the time of Buddha Shakyamuni. They've made important discoveries about the human mind. Nothing may be new as regards ultimate freedom, but in the relative ways in which we can understand how men and women are conditioned, rich discoveries have been made.

In the West some regard the teaching of the nonexistence of self to be a purely Oriental notion or simply an example of Buddhist bizarreness. It is true that we may find in the Buddhist tradition the clearest and most uncompromised expression regarding the absence of self. But all mystical traditions teach of the need to go beyond the self. Perhaps it is more striking when we find descriptions of self-transcendence outside purely spiritual circles. If the *I* does not truly exist it's not surprising that poets would give voice to this breathtaking lack.

Vision doesn't distinguish one artist from another so much perhaps as the way such vision finds expression. Skill and originality make each artist uncommon. And yet the vision of each artist must have a universal dimension. Some artists address their experiences in more explicit ways. In a book by Chuang Tzu I was surprised to find in the translator's introduction an excerpt from the French poet, Paul Valéry. I tried to learn more about him. Frequently, naturally, he experienced a sense of pure presence that he calls *pure self ("moi pur")*. He didn't formally practice any kind of meditation, and yet due to some inclination he had spiritual experiences. In his experience of *pure self* all sense of personality, of limit, disappears:

> *I only refer to my pure self by which I mean absolute consciousness, the unique and uniform means through which one turns loose from everything.*[4]

> *I freely compare this pure self to the precious zero of mathematical language.*[5]

> *...to feel the knowing itself and no object.*[6]

Painters may also express a deep vision of the world beyond appearances. Or rather they may see that the world is composed merely of appearances. Wandering one afternoon through the Museum of Modern Art in New York, I stopped—I was instantly riveted, spellbound—by a painting of Sainte Victoire Mountain, by Paul Cézanne. The canvas of the painting was in plain sight. It was as if the painting had not been entirely finished; it was as if the landscape and the space within which it appeared had merged with one another. The illusory nature of the landscape was apparent. Finally, I turned away and went to the cafeteria to ponder my experience. I tried to figure out what could lead an artist to such depth of perception.

Painters during Cézanne's time looked at landscapes for hours. Such intense gazing may lead painters to intuitively question the nature of the world. Sometimes the seer may even disappear through such intense gazing. What does seeing reveal? The landscape, the world itself, may suddenly appear to be of a different nature, with a different flavor. Cézanne himself said, "If I think while I am painting, if I intervene with the process, everything falls apart, all is lost."

Conventional ways of seeing must be seen through in order for artists to be more intimate with the world. Cézanne's pursuit is akin to a spiritual quest, as is the case for many artists. I remember a line by Paul Klee:

> In this world, no one can grasp me for my abode is as much in the world of the dead as in the world of the unborn. A little closer to the heart of creation than is customary. And yet, still much too far.[7]

Is not the heart of creation the depth of the mind, one's original mind, as the Zen tradition calls it?

Writers are fascinated by the place where words form, the silence from which all words arise. For some writers, silence and words are as merged, as inseparable as the landscape and empty canvas of Cézanne's painting. Words cannot really pass beyond the silence of their origin.

Maurice Blanchot, Georges Bataille, Samuel Beckett—I've found many enlightening reflections in the work of those modern writers. Questioning the space of writing, they reveal the illusory, and yet very real power of words.

> The writer belongs to a language that no one speaks, which is addressed to no one, which has no center, and which reveals nothing.[8]

Blanchot also said: "to write is to surrender to the fascination of time's absence."

What does it mean—a language which reveals nothing? When Cézanne painted Sainte Victoire Mountain he didn't so much show a mountain as disclose his vision. When a writer composes fiction, tells a story about people, she creates characters, places, times that have no reality whatsoever. But some writers, in their own genuine way, disclose the unreality of their fiction. They explore and reveal the source whence creation takes shape, not unlike meditators investigating the origin of their thoughts. Their skill lies not in the making of believable stories, but in the way their stories give nothing for their reader to grasp.

In the Buddhist scriptures there is a text, dating to perhaps the fourth century, which seems strikingly modern: the *Vimalakirtinirdesha Sutra*. It describes the unreality of the world, its empty nature. The doctrine's exponent isn't the Buddha, but rather an enigmatic figure, the layman Vimalakirti. His wisdom is so bright that no one dares to approach him, even the most revered disciples of the Buddha. Only one bodhisattva finally engages in a discussion with him.

Vimalakirti's teaching is rife with paradox:

> *When a Bodhisattva follows the wrong way, he follows the way to attain the qualities of the Buddha.*[9]

And while the text is not always consistent in such respects, at times Vimalakirti is a baffling, impossible character. He has a wife and son, and yet he is celibate. He appears to be surrounded by servants, and yet he lives in solitude. Contradiction has also been abundantly used by modern writers. Maurice Blanchot, for example, describes his main character in *The Last Man* in this way:

> *As if there were of him only presence and it wouldn't allow him to be present: vast presence, himself seemingly unable to fill it, as if he had disappeared within it, and it had absorbed him slowly, eternally, a presence with no one, maybe.*[10]

This could be a perfect description of Vimalakirti as well and of the truth that he represents.

We don't explore in the practice of Gesture of Awareness how the world of form merges with space or how words blend ineluctably with silence. We explore how physical sensations never depart from the nature of awareness. The body is the main place of inquiry in Gesture of Awareness. The body knows itself not as this sensation, or as that sensation, but as pure presence. As Meister Eckhart said, the soul is the place where God knows himself.

Early on, the body played a major role in the practice of Buddhist meditation. In the *Sattipatana Sutta* it is said:

> *Furthermore, when walking, the monk discerns that he is walking. When standing, he discerns that he is standing. When sitting, he discerns that he is sitting. When lying down, he discerns that he is lying down. Or however his body is disposed, that is how he discerns it.*

Later Buddhist traditions, however, fascinated by other aspects of spiritual life such as rituals, visualizations, and investigations into the nature of consciousness, put the body aside. The body was no longer viewed as a powerful locus for awakening, but seems to have been viewed with contempt. Yet all sensory fields are commonly used in Buddhism to discover not the nature of the object but the nature of the perceiving subject.

If the sensory experience of hearing can be a skillful means of awakening, so can other fields of sensory experience. Why wouldn't we realize our true nature by inquiring into the nature of bodily sensations?

The Chinese and Korean Buddhist traditions employ meditation on hearing as a skillful means of awakening to the mind's true essence. Such means predate the advent of Buddhism in China. We find an example of this in the Taoist tradition:

> *"What is the fasting of the mind?" Yen Houai asked Confucius. And Confucius said, "Unify your attention. Do not listen with your ears*

but with your mind; do not listen with your mind but with your essence. The ears can not do more than to listen, the mind can not do more than to recognize. As for the essence it is a void completely unengaged. The way gathers only in this void. This void is the fasting of the mind.[11]

There are numerous accounts of Buddhist masters who use hearing to lead disciples into discovery of their true nature. Chinul, founder of the Zen tradition in Korea, led students to realization of their true nature in such a way:

Chinul: You should know that what is capable of seeing, hearing, moving, and acting has to be your original mind; it is not your physical body. I will indicate one approach which will allow you to return to the source. Do you hear the sounds of that crow cawing and that magpie calling?

Student: Yes.

Chinul: Trace them back and listen to your hearing-nature. Do you hear any sounds?

Student: At that place, sounds and discriminations do not obtain.

Chinul: Marvelous! Marvelous! This is Avalokiteshvara's method for entering the noumenon. Let me ask you again. You said that sounds and discriminations do not obtain at that place. But since they do not obtain, isn't the hearing-nature just empty space at such a time?

Student: Originally it is not empty. It is always bright and never obscured.

Chinul: What is this essence which is not empty?

Student: As it has no former shape, words cannot describe it.[12]

A meditation that finds expression in mindfulness of the body is not concerned with an objective knowledge, but rather, as in all Buddhist traditions, with a way to know oneself deeply and be free.

So much importance in our present-day culture is given to the body, but to the body as object, not as subject. The body as seen by others, and not as it is, a body experienced in intimacy. We are concerned with the body we own and not with the body we are. Seeing the body in this way, we may find that it is rather like a cage in which our mind, or our soul, to use Christian terminology, is kept captive. But when deep intimacy with the body is developed, the cage-like body dissolves in the space-like mind.

Many mystical traditions teach that the body does not limit the mind but rather is simply an amalgam of phenomena experienced by the mind. For the Indian Guru Ramana Maharshi, the body is just a thought. Some Buddhist traditions would say that it is just the play of awareness. Such a statement, though, is not to be understood as a negation of external phenomena as notions of what may constitute inner and outer are the mere play of awareness.

According to Meister Eckhart, the body is more in the soul than the soul is in the body. Clear perception of the experience of the soul through the body isn't something one necessarily expects from Christian philosophers, many of whom tend to consider the body as a source of evil. Some masters teach that the soul is essentially in the heart but this isn't so, Meister Eckhart said, and they are mistaken in such respect. The soul is completely and totally undivided in the foot, in the eye, in any member of the body.

For a meditator who devotes attention to the body, whether in sitting or walking meditation, it may be of benefit to learn what other people in other contexts have to say about awareness of the body. Observing people walking across a meditation hall, I noticed how the walker's quality of presence can captivate the attention of the observer. It was not long before I turned to the world of actors and dancers to learn how they approach this aspect of their art. I found inspiration.

There was a performance by Bill T. Jones in Paris. Walking slowly to the middle of the stage—there was no music, only the man walking, naked. The intensity of the situation was vivid. Nothing else was needed. I imagine that he wasn't thinking, but simply and completely walking. If he'd been lost in his thoughts, there wouldn't have been a dance performance. It all seemed easy, natural. Later I learned in an interview that this wasn't so. He explained how risk itself was essential to him.

Jerzy Grotowski, the Polish theater director, worked with actors for months, even years, without being preoccupied by any need to present a show to an audience. He compelled the actors to undertake rigorous training, and they were transformed by it into spiritual seekers of a kind. The skill of the actors arose from their quality of mindfulness, one that is similar to the practice of meditation. Grotowski's notion of a total act was also deeply interesting to me. "I mean the very crux of the actor's art: that what the actor achieves should be a total act that he does whatever he does with his entire being..."[13] I'm well aware of the difference in perspective between performer and meditator. But as presence is not all there is to meditation, I likewise assume it's only one of many qualities needed by an actor, and yet it is an essential one.

Dancers spend thousands of hours in the practice of walking, standing, leaping, moving. They have developed a deep knowledge of the experience of the body and a vocabulary to express it. They may also certainly face the problems that can arise when any dichotomy between body and mind is made. "When we say that the actor/dancer uses her body, we may wonder," Eugenio Barba said in his essay, "The Credible Body." That is, we may wonder who is using what.

The experience of the unity between the inner dimension and the physical/mechanical dimension is not the starting point but the achievement of the work of the actor/dancer.

> The actor proceeds from the outer to the inner as if the body were a separate entity which the mind and the will can manipulate artificially. The approach consists in taking a path which at the beginning goes in the opposite direction of the aim wanted... The actor

who has accepted completely the illusion of duality and has over-come it acquires a second nature. When she assimilates this second nature without needing anymore to direct her consciousness as would a pilot, then the intention and the action, the mind and the body, cannot be distinguished. The body becomes unusual, striking, yet credible.[14]

The body of the accomplished dancer, the master, becomes "a body of presence and attention" as the French dancer and choreographer Dominique Dupuy said.

When we develop true intimacy with our body, we become intimate with ourselves. We learn to be present as a whole. We open to discovery of our essence when the dichotomy of body-mind is dropped.

That is precisely the purpose of the practice of Gesture of Awareness.

In this practice we explore movement to discover the nature of awareness. We inquire even of the sensation of tension in the neck—becoming aware not of the sensation but of the consciousness of it; becoming aware not of the consciousness of it, but of the essence of the consciousness. One does not always have to practice Gesture of Awareness, though, in such a gradual way.

If the body is just a thought, the play of awareness, then ultimately an intimate knowledge of the body is an intimate knowledge of awareness.

It is skillful to use the body as a means of inquiry into one's true essence. Buddhism has a long tradition of employing meditation on sound, but sounds flicker. They're unstable; they're dependent on external conditions. This is much less the case with the body. But in order to explore one's true essence one needs to stop elaborating on what is happening; one needs to let go of the habitual tendencies of judging, evaluating, of labeling every experience.

It is hard to lead classes without any suggestion of what a given experience should be. To lead classes in an ever open way. We're so used to modifying our experiences that the bare mention of one kind of experience may draw us on to try to transform or improve what is happening—thereby drawing us out from the experience. If asked, for example, "Can you be aware of your breath?" some participants may notice that their breath feels contrived, and immediately try to improve it. If asked, "Can you let the breath be contrived or free?" participants may interfere much less with their experience.

I've noticed when teaching meditation how often I, too, perpetuate a sense of time and duration. We're often too casual, too loose, in our way of speaking. First, second, or third day has no meaning with respect to present experience.

What does it mean to sit or to walk for fifteen minutes, or for an hour, from the point of view of being present? Language is conceived from the point of view of the experience and the experiencer, from the point of view of duality. When exploring modes of being, language can mislead us.

Sometimes I've noticed when participants work together in groups of three how each would take for granted that he or she would be in the middle during the next turn. They take this for reality. I bring this reality into question by stopping the exercise after two participants have had their turn in the middle, leaving one with their expectations unfulfilled. In *Lama Yangthig*, by the fourteenth-century Tibetan master Longchenpa, I found a similar instance. Here, the teacher asks the student to walk to a place some distance away. When the student has reached the midway point, the teacher asks the student to stop, and to return. This surprises the student and leaves him thoughtless, free of conceptualization.

The practice of Gesture of Awareness is, at times, akin to a koan. A koan not based on words but on situation. Not asking, "What is the sound of one hand clapping?," but asking rather, for example, when walking, "Can we be at two places at the same time, and if we have time, why not?" Many aspects of this practice find their source in Buddhist sutras like the *Sattipatana Sutta* and the *Bahia Sutta*. References can also be found in the texts of the great Indian commentators. As Nagarjuna, the illustrious teacher and commentator on the Buddha's teachings, says:

Walking does not start
In the steps taken or to come
Or in the act itself.
Where does it begin?
Before I raise a foot,
Is there motion,
A step taken or to come
Whence walking could begin?[15]

When asked what the writing of James Joyce was all about, Beckett said that it wasn't about something, but rather was the thing itself. I imagine the same could be said of Gesture of Awareness.

Each chapter is as the unfolding of a session of Gesture of Awareness. At the beginning, I question some aspects of what we take to be the reality of our experiences so that all participants including me may be drawn into a state of perplexity, into a mood of investigation. Some hunting tribes used to perform a dance before going off on their expeditions as a way of tuning in to the spirit of the hunt. I see the questioning at the beginning of a session as a dance of inquiry. And after, we explore through movement, gesture, and contact the truth of each moment. I lead participants in a kind of guided meditation through the practice of Gesture of Awareness.

This book is an account of those inquiry dances and of the meditative practices that follow.

Notes

1 Simone Weil, *Gravity and Grace* (Lincoln: University of Nebraska Press, 1997), 100.
2 Jean Piaget, *The Child's Conception of the World* (Lanham, Maryland: Littlefield Adams Quality Paperback, 1951), 33.
3 Jean Piaget, *The Child's Conception of the World*, 34.
4 G. Lanfranchi, *Paul Valéry et l'Expérience du MOI PUR*, translated by Charles Genoud (Paris: la Bibliothèque des Arts, 1993) 11.
5 G. Lanfranchi, *Paul Valéry et l'Expérience du MOI PUR*, 12.
6 G. Lanfranchi, *Paul Valéry et l'Expérience du MOI PUR*, 23.

7   Paul Klee, *Paul Klee Par Lui-Même et Par Son Fils Félix Klee* (Paris: Librairie Asso-
ciées, 1963), 1.

8   Maurice Blanchot, *The Space of Literature,* translated by Ann Smock (Lincoln: Uni-
versity of Nebraska Press, 1982), 26.

9   Vimalakirti, *The Holy Teaching of Vimalakirti,* translated by R. A. F. Thurman
(Pennsylvania: Pennsylvania State University Press, 1976), 64.

10   Maurice Blanchot, *Le Dernière Homme,* translated by Charles Genoud (Paris: Gal-
limard, 1957), 50–51.

11   J. F. Billeter, *Leçons sur Tchouang-tseu* (Paris: Allia Edition, 2002), 96.

12   R. E. Buswell, *Tracing Back the Radiance* (Honolulu: University of Hawaii, 1992), 104.

13   Jerzy Grotowski, *Toward a Poor Theatre* (London: Methuen Drama, 1968), 91.

14   Eugenio Barba, *Le Corps en Jeu* (Paris: CNRS Edition, 1994), 251–252.

15   Nagarjuna, *Nagarjuna, Verses from the Center,* translated by Stephen Batchelor (New
York: Riverhead Books, 2001), 84.

THE PAST NEVER WAS

The past never was.
   When I read this line
   by Maurice Blanchot, it disturbed me.

It left me gasping. It stopped my mind.
   Nothing more is happening
   than right now.

Nothing other will ever happen
   than right now.

Joseph Campbell writes
   of the quest for knowledge—
   of the hero's journey,

and the shaman's.
   Though chosen by destiny at birth
   the hero forgets it; he leads

an ordinary life among other people.
   One day, something reminds him, an event,
   and it prompts him into his journey.

It can be heavenly messengers,
   as happened for the Buddha,
   or it can be something less obvious.

It can be something
   suddenly out of place
   in the order of the world—

a cup set upside down,
   an open door normally closed,
   a sudden illness—

this breaches
   the shaman's world.
   This small thing

suddenly ruins
   not the thing itself,
   but the order of the world.

The world is not
   as the shaman
   once envisioned it;

something
   impossible happened.
   Ordinary people do not notice

the breaches;
   they want their world
   to be firm.

But the shaman
   is dedicated to knowledge; he can't
   ignore them.

But now he faces
   an incoherent world.
   Ordinary life has lost its interest;

he is anxious
   to find a vaster vision
   of the world,

a vision
   that includes the seemingly
   impossible.

To find it, the shaman
　　must now begin
　　his spiritual journey.

If we trusted someone,
　　completely,
　　and discovered one day

that this person lied to us,
　　from then on we would not trust
　　what this person says.

Maurice Blanchot didn't say
　　the past is no more, he said
　　the past never was.

We may imagine
　　that if the past never was,
　　the future will never be.

And yet, life for us
　　appears to have duration.

There is a gap of time
　　between yesterday
　　and two thousand years ago.

If the past never was
　　there is no gap of time.
　　The stretch of time between one date

and another is just a thought, a mere dream.
　　Yet memories
　　can seem so vivid.

What is brought back through memory?
　　Experiences can't be stored, brought
　　back to mind—only images can.

To remember,
   we record our experiences
   through images and concepts;

we step from the experience
   to the image of the experience.

It is as if our mind were taking
   a picture of each
   of our experiences.

What we call a past experience
   was never an experience,
   only an image.

The past never was
   anything other
   than a present image.

When we believe
   life has duration—

having time
   or not having time
   bind equally.

Considering that the past
   may never have been
   provides

a dramatic shift
   in our life. It doesn't simply
   question our belief

in the past, it questions
   our entire vision
   of the world:

the world begins to fall apart.
   Between a non-existing
   past and a non-existing future,

is there any time
   for something to happen?

Does the present exist?
   We may forget Blanchot's line—
   the past never was—

we may dismiss it as senseless,
   or we may embark
   on a spiritual journey.

Answering the call
   to shamanhood

may mean to slip through
   the breach
   into an unknown world.

A world in which the notion
   of time
   is absent.

can you come up to standing

can you move your arm
from left
to right
in front of you

just feel
the movement

feel the weight
of your arm moving

can you move your arm
from right
to left

now in the past

move your arm
in the past

you may try

move your arm
from left
to right
in the past

now in the future

can you do it
in the future

move your arm
from left
to right
in the future

can we

make a movement
in the past

make a movement
in the future

then explore
the movement
in the present

from left
to right

from right
to left

experience the presence
of a movement

you may walk

ACTOR

At a meditation retreat, we may think
   we're concerned with meditation,
   but we may simply be concerned with life.

If meditation takes us away from life,
   what is the use of meditation?

Do we attend a retreat
   to learn a technique,
   an exotic practice we can take home—

a practice that gives us
   the feeling we've got something,

a rare practice
   that most people have
   never heard of?

Maybe practice
   makes us feel special.

But if we don't understand ourselves,
   life, through meditation,
   what's the use of it?

Is meditation yet another way
   to distract ourselves from life?

Don't we look sometimes for the wrong things—
   more information, perhaps—
   to help us later on?

I wondered before one retreat
   whether I should do
   something new.

"If I don't do something new," I thought,
   "students who've already practiced with me
   might think we're repeating things."

But what things would I repeat?
   How could one bring something old?
   From where?

Gesture of Awareness is useless,
   and the useless cannot be old.

If our movements were useful
   they could be completed;
   they could become old.

If I needed to paint
   a building white, for example, I'd do it:
   we'd see consequences.

To paint and repaint a white building,
   though, would be silly,
   and so I don't.

As the gestures we're exploring
   are completely useless,
   they leave no traces.

We cannot say
   the gestures have been done,
   that they're over.

What we're exploring
   is not something useful.

We're not exploring anything to get
    or to become,
    but rather just being,

being at every instant.
    Nothing from the past,
    nothing from the future.

It's not what we may do that's important,
    it's the doing of it.

We may repeat exactly the same gesture,
    just as those Thai monks who practice
    meditation by moving their arm up and down,

up and down, the monks
    keeping on for hours, days,
    months, years.

It seems the practice increases
    their wisdom, provided they don't
    hold to what they've already done,

provided they don't hold to the wish
    to compare two gestures,
    or to improve their movements.

Provided they don't hold
    to anything.

Once, in Paris I met
    with an excellent actor
    in Peter Brooks' company.

I hoped he might be interested
    in Gesture of Awareness.

We spoke
    for some time
    in a restaurant.

He had the same quality of presence
　　chatting with me as he had onstage
　　in a leading role before a large audience.

It wasn't as if he'd been playing,
　　and now, between performances,
　　was wasting time.

After we'd finished speaking, he made sure
　　everything—our tables and chairs and so on—
　　was back in its place as when we arrived,

and only then did he leave
　　to rest before
　　his next performance.

There was no hierarchy
　　of activity.

Every instant was
　　just what one has.
　　Every instant was all.

Gesture of Awareness isn't
　　organized and codified;
　　it's no formal meditation.

And yet Gesture of Awareness is concerned
　　with the same sense of being
　　as in meditation:

being present at every instant.
　　Being present in what is essential.

Gesture of Awareness
　　isn't concerned with the contents
　　of what is happening.

It isn't concerned
    with thoughts, or emotions,
    or any specific sensations.

To be interested in the contents
    of whatever is happening is fine,

and yet there may be something
    more essential in just being present,
    something more primordial.

We explore different
    positions, gestures,
    subtle touching with another.

Can we be open
    in our meditation—

can we be open
    as we walk or touch another?
    What does it mean to be open?

Does it mean to simply
    have one's eyes open?

I give instructions
    in an open way so as not to interfere
    with your experience;

I question the habitual
    patterns toward which we may
    be easily drawn.

It's not up to me to decide
    what will happen for you
    or for me.

Rather, I leave space
    for anything to happen.

You're seated, and quiet,
   and ready for good meditation,

but now I've come to ask you
   to get rid of all your well-made plans
   so that we may explore something other.

There are professional meditators
   who can sit quietly for hours, but now
   I'm disturbing everything.

Can you remove
   the meditation cushion?

you may walk

just be walking

can you be
at two places at
the same time

you may try

be at two places at
the same time

you may walk
slowly or
fast

but be at two places
at the same time

if you can't

then be
every instant
in one place

you may stop

you may let your eyes close and
just be
standing

experiencing

nothing to change

nothing to improve

can we feel the floor
beneath our feet

feel its
temperature

feel its
texture

is it hard or
soft

cold

warm

can we just be
standing

without interfering

without changing anything

without keeping anything

feeling how heavy
or light
you are

can I be

can I stand

as a way
of being

a simple way
of being

you may walk

and stop

and see

where has your walking
gone

you may walk

where has your standing
gone

you may move

and stop

and know

where has your moving
gone

can we be moving and
standing still
at the same time

you may try

explore

moving

stopping
moving
at the same time

you may stop

close your eyes

can you slightly
lift
your shoulders

slightly

maybe an inch
or so

and feel
what is happening
within yourself

being open or
not to what
is happening

respect what you feel

slowly let them
come down

feel the way
the shoulders
come down

we're not interested
in having shoulders
down or up

but rather

in the movement
of life that
manifests

while moving our shoulders
down or up

can you lift
your shoulders

you can leave them up

and feel what's happening
within yourself

slowly let them
down

standing

open your eyes

and just walk as a way
of being

not
going
anywhere

TAKING RISKS

In the practice of Gesture of Awareness,
   we do not cultivate images, concepts,
   which could veil reality.

Those veils are like the dust
   on the window of a moving car
   as the sun sets on the horizon,

the landscape so mixing
   with the diffused and dusky light
   one may not see the road.

Stories that arise as one
   is just standing or touching another
   may be like that diffused light,

the dust of our preoccupation
   so veiling the situation we see
   neither ourselves nor others.

Sometimes, our images, our dreams are simple:
   we're by the sea dreaming of the mountains,
   or we're in class dreaming that it's over—

the concept of time, and the separation
   of subject and object, are the dust
   that veils many of our experiences.

If I were to ask you
   to walk for five minutes
   you'd understand what I mean.

We'd both be taken in
    by the notion of time,

by the belief in duration.
    Some Buddhist meditation
    traditions have practices
    not based on causality.

It's not by gathering causes
    that an unconditioned result
    will be reached;

it's not by looking for freedom
    that freedom
    will be found.

Looking for something binds us
    in time; it keeps us from being
    in touch with reality.

We may tune in to the same attitude
    by not setting up some aim
    toward which we may advance—

not looking for something,
    not finding something.

But what to do when we're not looking,
    when we're not finding?

Don't most of us engage in looking
    for something, even small things?
    It's easy to check

if one is looking for something—
    by asking if one is only looking for
    something that is missing.

Is anything missing?
  Let's see the practice
  from another angle:

if we consider practitioners,
  meditators who've been practicing
  for a long time,

why is it that some meditators
  seem to express
  a sense of inner freedom,

and why is it that some meditators
  seem as confused and unhappy
  as those without spiritual practice?

If spiritual paths
  have any effects,
  it's not due to years of practice.

It's important to question
  what does make for difference.

What does make way for change or not
  may have to do
  with the willingness to change.

It may have something to do
  with the willingness
  to take risks.

Is it possible to engage in a spiritual path
  without taking the risk
  to put oneself on the line?

When we want to stay protected,
  don't we protect the very thing
  that needs to be questioned?

We may be diligent, spending
   months and years engaged in practice,
   but be unwilling to put ourselves on the line.

The question is not whether
   we risk this or that. Rather,
   it's our being we put at risk.

What does it mean
   to put oneself in the game?

In the tradition of meditation, the set-up creates
   a space protected from outside intrusion,
   a skillful means.

And yet, if one carries this protection within,
   isn't the space of meditation
   a space of stagnation?

In Gesture of Awareness
   the set-up isn't one of protection.

When we work with another person
   we are spontaneously
   more attentive.

I've never seen someone
   move the arm or hand
   of another person carelessly.

We are naturally more present,
   and more exposed.

Does the willingness to change
   mean that the practitioner
   has in mind a picture of some future state:

the practitioner open to new possibility
   as she selects the future?
   But this new state is only an imagined state.

Isn't this how we spend our lives:
   trying to select the future?

And isn't trying to select the future
   what makes us live
   in dreams, in fictions?

The willingness to change
   may not be the wish to change.

The willingness to change is rooted
   in the acceptance of what is.
   What is can only be present.

The wish to change is rooted
   in the what should be, and can only
   be made of past or future images.

Willingness to change
   doesn't mean choosing the future.
   Rather it means being present

in an open way,
   not anticipating
   what could happen next,

and not holding on
   to what is happening.

The willingness to change
   may be the risk to be present
   without clinging.

Sometimes we may feel
   the need to be protected
   and that's fine.

If we choose, we may participate in class
   by sitting in a corner,
   just listening.

The freedom to not join in
    is important—
    explore it if you like.

It's not easy
    to take a risk.

In Geneva I joined
    a spiritual group
    connected to a temple in Brazil.

The *Babalorisha** came once a year
    for a few weeks to train
    the participants,

and sometimes the participants would go
    to Brazil to enhance
    their practice.

The group would meet
    Monday evenings for a ritual.

During the ritual,
    the participants would channel spirits
    who speak through them.

Every Monday for two years
    I went as an outsider,
    just to look.

I began to dance
    and sing the ritual songs,
    yet still I kept some distance away.

I went as far
    as I was prepared to go.

*spiritual leader in Afro-Brazilian traditions

One day, the Babalorisha arrived from Brazil
    and he told me to make up my mind
    to join fully or not come at all.

I was perplexed, but then I realized
    the only reason for me to not join in
    was fear, the fear of being exposed, or of taking a risk,

and that was true
    not only in this instance,
    but throughout my spiritual practice.

I'd been pretending to follow a spiritual path.
    I'd been avoiding
    having to put myself on the line.

So I went again,
    and when the Babalorisha put his hand
    on my forehead, I began to spin.

I couldn't stop,
    for if I stopped I'd fall.
    My training had started.

you may walk in the hall

can you feel
the floor
beneath you

can you feel
the floor
at each step

its temperature

its hardness or
softness

are you following
some pattern

walking in
some circle

you may change
direction

you may stop
and let your eyes
close

can you feel
the floor beneath your feet

can you feel
the space you occupy

from your feet
all the way
to your head

you may move
very slightly
shifting the weight
of the body onto
the right leg

feel
what is happening

some sensation
may arise

come to the center

and shift the weight
of your body
to the left

to the center

I almost said
back to the center

of course there is no
going back
it is impossible
to re-experience
the past

you may let
your eyes
open slowly

and take
a first step

the first in
this instant

can you take
a second step

now we are
standing
where is the last
step

can we experience it
again

can we bring it
back

now we are
standing
where is the next
step

can we experience it
already

can we take two steps
at the same time

can we experience
the next
step

you may walk

we may know where we are
by our contact with the floor

feeling the floor

this is where I am

place your hand
on your head

feel the space you occupy between the floor
and your hand

that is exactly the limit
to which one may experience
one's physical being

between the floor and the hand
not more

you may take
your hand away

the pull of gravity ever acts
upon us

it reveals where
we stand

you may move your hands
your arms
in front of you

they have some weight

you may feel where they are at
every instant

don't be misled by words

when I say
where are your hands

it's also where
you are

you may let your arms answer
the call of the earth
and let them go down slowly

you may lie down
on the floor

resting on the floor
as a way of being

SLAVE

Attending a retreat requires sacrifice.
  We need money and time to get away
  from our family and our work.

A few people are willing to make this sacrifice.
  We may wonder why they do,
  and what it is they expect.

In daily life we all have work to do.
  Perhaps we are efficient
  as we organize ourselves,

and come evening, if we have been efficient
  through the day, we may be satisfied,
  even full of pride.

Perhaps our efficiency will be rewarded
  with a higher salary.

In accomplishing work it doesn't matter
  with respect to the work itself
  if we feel well or not.

Later, when we consider the work we've done,
  we won't remember whether we felt well,
  we'll just contemplate the result.

Our days are organized by what
  we wish to accomplish and this may be imposed
  upon us by ourselves or another.

Our days are directed by whatever needs doing—
though house-painting, for example, doesn't much
reveal the inner life of the painter.

Our daily life is made subject to a result,
and thus it is conditioned.

In antiquity slaves
were treated as objects.

For some Greek masters it came as a shock
to learn their slaves
were afraid of dying.

It was as if a tool suddenly had a will of its own,
its own project.

Citizens of Athens could hope for life
after death, but not so the slaves—
their being resided in their usefulness.

When we bind ourselves to the accomplishment
of a task are we not transforming ourselves
into animated tools—into slaves?

The preeminence, the ruling factor
of work to be done, leaves no room
for the being of the doer.

Being master and slave at once,
twice bound,
and proud of such an accomplishment.

When we meditate, we may include
our concern for efficiency,
seeing our practice as a means to an end.

Are we not transforming ourselves
into tools, binding ourselves to a result,
and even calling the result *freedom*.

Can we practice without binding
    ourselves to any result? Can we practice
    without waiting for any future result?

Someone enters the meditation hall and sits down,
    gets up, and leaves.
    Nothing has been accomplished.

Maybe this person did not expect a deep experience,
    didn't apprehend anything,
    had no purpose whatsoever.

Can we bring this simplicity to our practice
    and not bargain with it,
    saying whatever?

Saying, I will be present when I'm fine,
    when I don't need to change anything,
    and all my expectations have been fulfilled.

Isn't this very attempt to attain
    anything bondage?

Likewise the challenge for me.
    Can I write without intention?
    Can I lead a class without purpose,

without trying to teach? In telling you
    not to reduce yourself to a tool
    am I not making a speaking tool of myself?

Why is it some of us don't change?
    What is it that provokes us to repeat the same
    binding patterns?

Isn't this related to not taking the risk—
    the risk to be present?

Instead, we cling to the wish
    to improve things.

There are meditators who sit quietly as long as no one
    disturbs them or comes close,
    and it's fine to like feeling protected.

Sometimes, though, we might challenge that sense
    of security. See whether we're willing to take the risk
    to interact with one another.

Take the risk to interact
    with one another in a clear way.

There is a subtle balance between
    taking a risk and respecting oneself:
    I respect myself enough to take a risk.

In the practice of Gesture of Awareness
    we do not sit quietly. We do
    interact with each another.

We even touch each other
    in a clear way.

Our mind might add stories,
    stories that are less clear, and that's fine.
    Why should we always have a clear mind?

Contacting another might be
    a challenge for some of us—
    the mind mixing experiences with stories.

The only one who can decide whether
    you are ready is you.
    Ready, in this instant.

Are you ready for the challenge?
    If you don't feel like doing some experiment,
    just don't.

Who is ready to risk?
   We don't know what to expect—
   that's a risk!

can you stand

can you move your arm
in front of you

just feel
the movement

feel the weight
of your arm moving

can you move your arm
from right
to left

now in the past

you may try

move your arm
in the past

now in the future

can we
make a movement
in the past

make a movement
in the future

then explore
the movement
in the present

from left
to right

experience the presence
of the movement

can we really
experience a movement

let's try

how much of the movement
can we experience
at a time

can we experience
the beginning
and the middle
at the same time

can we experience
the middle
and the end
at the same time

how much of the movement
can we experience at
a time

can our hand be at two places at
the same time

if not
if our hand is at one place
at a time

how is movement different
from stillness

how much of a movement
can we experience at
a time

try it

you may stop
bring your hand
in a position of rest

for how long are we going
to walk

does how long
mean anything at all

when did you start

you may stop

where has the walking gone

you may stop and make teams
of three people

one person will be in the center
and the others on either
the left or right

when the person in the center
is ready
that person will make a sign
by raising the right hand

those on the left and right will
delicately put
one hand on the shoulder
of the person in the center

the one in the center may feel
where she
or he stands

those on left and right
are not doing anything
to help
the one in the center

we're just exploring being
with the hand touching
another person

or being
standing

different ways of being

it's no better to be in the center
than on either
left or right

we're not concerned with the content
of our experiences
touching or being touched

feeling at ease
or not

we are concerned
with being
sometimes we may not feel
comfortable

can I be open to this
to the not liking

just being
standing

touching another person

being touched

thinking or not thinking

nothing to change
nothing to keep

being open or
not

up to where
do I feel this contact

just in my shoulders or do I feel it
in my chest also

does it affect
the way I breathe

respect what you feel

you may withdraw your hands

it's also a way of being
taking one's hands
away

how am I standing
now

how does it feel to be
standing

just standing

you may switch position

those on the left and right will
delicately put
one hand on the shoulder
of the person in the center

how far am I willing
to experience
being touched

just on my shoulders or am I
willing
to feel it completely

there's no need to change
anything

just being

does it affect the way
I breathe

does it affect the way
I stand

do I feel it
just on my shoulders or

am I feeling it
in my chest in my abdomen
in my feet

when I'm touching
another person's shoulder
does it affect the way
I breathe

can I let my breath
be free
or contrived

without transforming
anything

does it affect the way
I stand

when you feel it is enough
you may remove your hand

nothing is over
we still are

our being is not less or more
complete
when touching
another person

or when standing
alone

in this instant the only thing
that will ever happen for me
is just standing

now we may walk

walking
on the floor

it's amazing how difficult it is
to be present
yet it's impossible to be
in the past or in the future

we're tiring ourselves by trying
to do something

it's impossible
not to be

just be

walking

DANCE

Religions, archaic religions—
    it's striking to read that most religious acts
    are viewed by sociologists as useful.

Rites viewed from the standpoint of
    their profitability,
    their usefulness for the cohesion of the group,

as if such means
    were inherent in any activity.

As if human behavior
    can be reduced to profit.

For a mind entangled in becoming,
    it may be difficult
    to understand religious acts.

The homeless in the streets
    may be less likely to reduce everything
    to profit, to future consequences.

In a world where production plays
    an important role,

in a world where wholeness
    is sought through
    an accumulation of objects,

what way could there be
    out from this trap?

An act of no production.
   Not motionless meditation,
   but a de-producing act,

the dissipation of what one accumulates—
   an act of pure wasting.
   Sacrifice.

Sometimes animals are offered,
   sometimes food is wasted, but the ultimate
   sacrifice is any sense of purpose.

Meditation
   can be a sacrifice
   when one practices without reason,

when one practices without a why,
   as Meister Eckhart says.

Our practice is akin to sacrifice
   when that need
   to make sense is offered.

As it accomplishes nothing, as it leaves
   no trace, dance is associated
   with the oldest forms of sacrifice.

Animals dance to seduce a potential mate,
   or they transmit signs like bees,
   but none dance without purpose.

When dancers want
   to make beautiful movements
   they subject their art to something else;

they reduce themselves, their dancing
   to show, to mere appearances,
   to bondage.

Some dances, though, are performed
   without design, not subject to anything.
   They are just it.

Ultimate sacrifice,
   Shiva's devastating dance,
   is an act of pure de-creation.

A dance where all worlds
   dissipate within the consciousness
   of the whirling god,

a dance where no place
   of reference is left:
   neither motion nor stillness.

Practice in Gesture of Awareness
   is a dance,
   even if we don't move.

The end of production;
   the end of accumulation.
   The end of purpose.

you may walk

what we are doing

is completely useless

there is nothing
to do or
to undo

no failure

you may relax

no success either
you may relax

can you walk

and stop

you may walk

and stop

is stopping experienced
as an interruption of
something

walk

and stop

is stopping experienced
as an interruption of
something

sometimes one may feel the clinging
to an unaccomplished project
as a slight tension in the chest

you may walk

and stop

is stopping experienced
as an interruption
of an intention

just be standing

close your eyes

you may bring one hand
to your neck

one hand
to your forehead

just being
standing

does it affect the way
I stand

can you feel the effect
of the contact in
your chest

can you feel the effect
of the contact in
your abdomen

you may bring
your arms down

feel the temperature
of your fingers

if you wish you may
move them slightly

let your fingers feel
their own temperature

you may stop
moving your fingers

make a small movement
with your hips
to the right

to the left

feel the movement
to the left
back to

there is no going back

find a place of balance
in the middle

you may stop

you may walk

you may makes teams
of three persons

what are we going to do three by three
do you know

you're just standing
three by three
just that

what next

is there ever anything happening

next

is next ever happening

you may dissolve the teams

and walk

you may make teams of two persons

one person will
face the wall
one person will stand to the side
facing the other

when the person facing the wall
is ready
he or she will make a sign

the other will place hands
on the forehead
and on the neck
of the person facing the wall

nothing to transform

nothing to improve

to change

to keep

just a way of being
together

respect whatever you feel

feeling at ease

feeling not at ease

you may withdraw your hands

you may walk
in the hall

place one hand
on your head

walk

does it affect
the way I breathe

does it affect
the way I walk

you may withdraw
your hand

you may lie on the floor
on your back

maybe something is still
happening within ourselves

we're not concerned
with the body

we're concerned with
being present

can you trust the floor
to receive you

to support you

can you feel the floor through you

its temperature

its hardness

its softness

just rest on the back

SACRIFICE

Being, or being present,
    cannot be an aim.
    Otherwise it's in the future.

If we were to cultivate this aim,
    we'd keep ourselves within
    the framework of becoming.

Being cannot be
    in the future or in the past.

We may speak of the present,
    of being, but being doesn't need
    any concept of time.

When we speak of the present
    it's to avoid slipping
    into past or future.

Being cannot be
    an aim, an objective.

However hard we may try,
    however skillful we may be,
    to try anything places us

in the field of becoming,
    in the world of artifacts and tools,
    in the world of not being.

At some point, we may imagine
    someone took a stick and a stone
    and tied them together into a tool.

The stick and stone before the tool
    was made had their own being.

In the making of the tool,
    the wood lost its woodness
    and the stone its stoneness.

The stick and the stone
    became something other than themselves,
    existing only for some purpose.

Its own being lost,
    a tool exists to accomplish something
    other than itself.

After it has been used,
    when its purpose has disappeared,
    the tool is thrown away.

But not only the tool,
    but also its maker, and its user,
    are bound to a purpose.

As the wood lost its woodness
    and the stone its stoneness,
    we too may lose our being.

We may lose our being when we exist only
    for some purpose, for something
    other than ourselves.

To destroy efficiency,
    the *workerness* of the worker—
    to find their being—

men and women of old
    celebrated sacrifices.
    Being a function, a sentient tool—

a potter, hunter, carpenter,
   not a being in any case—those tool-makers
   and their sons and daughters,

grandsons and granddaughters,
   may have realized
   they had lost something essential;

they may have realized
   that something—their being—
   was lacking.

In the attempt to recapture their being,
   they tried to undo the doing
   of their tool-making.

They tried to initiate action
   that didn't bear fruit,
   that negates purpose.

They tried to undo their work,
   their own worker's efficiency
   annihilated.

When work and efficiency lead
   to accumulation of food and wealth
   the undoing of them

is expressed as waste.
   In the sacrifice, the worker
   becomes the sacrificer;

the worker takes
   what has been accomplished
   only to waste it, destroy it.

The worker destroys it
   as a rebellious act against
   becoming and time.

When reflecting on sacrifice,
  sociologists reduce it
  to usefulness.

They try to find some benefit
  for the tribe in sacrifice, perhaps something
  related to unity, or to prosperity.

But this material vision doesn't see through
  to the ultimate richness of waste.
  Being is of no concern.

Sacrifice takes the useful,
  the required effort,
  and wastes it, destroys it.

One can waste only
  what has been produced.

As they were not
  the result of purposeful action,
  the sacrifice of wild animals was uncommon,

as was the sacrifice of trees
  and plants. Their destruction would not be
  the undoing of some doing;

sacrifice is the opposite
  of efficiency, of artifact.

Sacrifice is the opposite
  of duration and time.

Those rites of sacrifice were experienced
  as though they were taking place in a primordial time,
  a timeless time.

There's the story of Chuang-Tzu
  walking with a disciple
  on a hilltop.

They see a crooked,
  ancient tree
  without a single straight branch.

The disciple says
  the tree is useless,
  nothing from it can be used,

and Chuang-Tzu says,
  "That's why it's an ancient tree."

We cultivate the attitude
  of efficiency in such way
  that we see the earth itself as a tool.

The earth as a tool,
  the ocean as a reservoir of food,
  and the forest a preserve of oxygen—

when we see the earth
  in a useful way
  we don't see it anymore.

We see only
  the benefit we wish for,

connecting with profit only.
  Disconnected from the earth,
  we're as aliens on our own planet.

In the practice of Gesture of Awareness,
  when we try to correct, to transform something,
  we reduce ourselves to a tool.

Lost in becoming,
  we cannot experience being.

Becoming more,
  or less, or better—
  becoming else in any case,

we can trick our mind.
   Just a little becoming,
   we might say.

But a little becoming is as far
   from being as a big becoming.

Just slightly improving my breath;
   just shifting my head in order to
   make use of useless action—

seeing the useless as useless for something,
   the sacrifice of an animal
   becomes simply the preparation of a meal,

the axe of sacrifice now blunted,
   edgeless.

Let's not make sense
   of the things we do.
   Let's sacrifice meaningfulness.

can you stand

   you may make teams of two persons
   one person in front and
   the other in back

   you may walk
   together

   those in front may change
   their mind

and walk fast
slow
not following any pattern

feel free to change
your mind

going to the left
or to the right

what is happening

one person walking in
front of another

if some in front try to
trick the ones behind

are they not
tricking themselves

are they not binding themselves to
the attempt
to trick the other person

can you walk freely
walking in front
walking behind
another person

not binding yourself

like a tool
like a worker

not only freedom in
a vast place

but freedom also
in a confined place

you may stop
find a place close to the wall
facing it

sometimes the mind is
anticipating
sometimes not

close your eyes

slowly bend your head
forward

slowly

until you touch the wall

can you be where you are
at every instant

where is the wall
when you're not touching it

just an image

not a sensation

a sensation has
lightness heaviness
softness roughness

does it have color
shape

when in contact with the wall
feel its temperature

can you feel it in
your forehead

your chest
your abdomen

can you feel the temperature of the wall
in your neck

when touching the wall

is there any distance
between yourself and the wall

you may walk

find a place to
rest on the floor

being in contact
with the floor

are you really in
contact with the floor

when we rest
on the floor

what distance could there be
between us and the floor

how far am I from
the floor

do you need to do anything to
lie on the floor

does it require any
doing
some making

if it doesn't require any
making
why do anything

if you'd like to make something
make it

usually one likes to be useful
to oneself

you may let both arms rest
on either side of you on the floor

lift your right arm a little

so little that anyone looking on
wouldn't see the movement

your arm is not completely in touch
with the floor

you may relax
your arm

let it rest
on the floor

just resting
on the floor

is it heavy

is it light

you may raise your left arm

raising it so little that anyone looking on
wouldn't notice

but you feel it

you may let your arm
or yourself rest
on the floor

how is your arm
resting on the floor

is it heavy
is it cold

carefully

roll onto your side slightly

being in contact
with the floor

you may just slightly roll over

and feel at every instant the contact
with the floor

very slowly roll over
and feel

which part of yourself
is in contact with the floor

slowly you may
stand

feel all the way up how
the pull of gravity
reveals where you are

the pull of gravity never fails
to assure
our contact with the floor

with the earth

RED SUNFLOWER

A red sunflower—
   is it possible?

It's enough to prove
   a red sunflower exists
   by revealing it.

To prove it does not exist
   would be
   more difficult.

Must we check
   each and every sunflower?

It would be easy for me
   to teach through demonstration
   ways of moving,

standing, lying down.
   We'd soon learn
to move in such and such a way.
   We could have a sense
   of accomplishment.

But we're not here
   to learn correct
   ways of moving.

Each experience is perfect
   in its actuality as there is nothing
   real to compare with it.

Is it possible, for example, to feel
    the temperature of a copper bowl
    just by looking at it?

Can one experience
    bodily sensations through
    an image?

One may observe
    the copper bowl at a distance,
    but not experience it.

We experience the world
    at a distance,
    mostly.

We experience the world through
    projections, fantasies, and hence,
    without intimacy.

Generally we don't leave
    our experiences as they are.
    Rather, we look for improvement.

Trying to improve a sensation
    is costly.

For small benefit,
    for partial improvement,
    we sacrifice our completeness.

In order to judge an experience
    we step outside it,
    dividing ourselves.

We're not ambitious
    if we spend our life
    trying to improve it.

The totality of our being can be realized
   only when we're totally with
   the experience happening now.

It requires the absence
   of movement toward anything
   not happening now.

If we need to part from anything
   to find completeness
   we limit ourselves.

Partial completeness,
   an incomplete completeness—

completeness
   is not constructed, is not
   dependent on any situation outside it.

Nothing lies outside
   of completeness.

It is the way
   we experience,
   and not what we experience.

Completeness, perfection,
   is what we start with,
   not what we aim for.

Perfection, as nothing is lacking;
   perfection, as nothing is apart from it;
   perfection, as nothing can be added to it.

If nothing
   can be added,
   it has no use for usefulness.

The practice of Gesture of Awareness is
   perfectly useless.

Perfection
    is not the aim.
    It's happening now.

you may stand

can you let your eyes close

just be standing

can you feel the way
you stand

you may place your hands
on the sides of your head

bend the upper part of your body
to the left

to the right

to the center

can you let your breath
be free
or contrived

without changing
anything

place one hand on your neck
and the other hand
on your forehead

how far are you willing
to be touched

nothing to improve

nothing to transform

carefully bring
your hands
to rest by your legs

you may let your eyes open slowly
let the visual field
come through you
as through a window

forget the image
just be seeing

you may walk

walk fast
at one place at a time
unless you like to be at two

I imagine
we hear in a different way

slightly

at each place

just be aware
of the sounds going through you

forget about the image
just let hearing hear

you don't need to hear
hearing does it

is hearing happening
anywhere

when there is just hearing
does here
have any meaning

you may stop

find a place to rest on the floor

rest on the back

you may bring one hand
to your forehead

how far are you willing
to be touched

can you let your breath
be free
or contrived

bring your hand to rest
on the floor

very slightly lift both arms

let the right one come down
to rest on the floor

let the left one come down
to rest on the floor

just be resting

on the floor

I IS ANOTHER

Meister Eckhart
  played free with his sources.

Sermonizing,
  he'd take a line from the Bible
  and misquote it,

interpreting
  as he liked.
  The text as pretext.

Rimbaud's line
  I is another
  could be our pretext.

Revealing
  what places
  completeness out of reach—

I is another is a striking
  assertion.

Let's consider one way of looking
  at the development
  of a young child.

At first, a newborn has no sense
  of separateness,
  no sense of self and other,

of I and mother.
  The infant lives with a sense
  of limitlessness,

an oceanic feeling.
   Through hours of gazing
   into the mother's eyes

individuality gradually develops.
   The mother's eyes
   become the mirror

through which the infant
   begins to perceive
   itself.

In time, the infant
   shares the mother's conviction
   that it is a separate being,

seeing itself as the mother does
   from the outside,
   as if separate from itself.

We look at ourselves
   the way our parents did,
   and the way they looked at others:

We experience ourselves
   from the point of view
   of other.

Fragmented,
   we live at a distance
   from our life.

When I see,
   is *I* one thing
   and *seeing* another thing?

When I feel a bodily sensation,
   is *I* one thing
   and *feeling* another thing?

If the *I* can see,
   why does it need seeing?

If the *I* can't see,
   why does seeing need it?

Death reveals the imposture
   of this fragmentation.

We fear our death
   as if we were someone
   very dear;

we fear our death
   because we are attached
   to ourselves,

but who is attached
   to whom?

When we fear the death of someone,
   we dread their lack,
   their absence.

My fear of death
   is the fear of the lack
   that my demise unveils.

But will I be there
   to experience this lack,
   to face my absence?

Is I another?

Oneness cannot be learned
   from outside,
   from other.

It must be
   discovered within.

The experience, the sense
   of oneness, is important in all
   mystical traditions.

This doesn't mean, though,
   that traditions are limited
   by this sense of oneness.

A Sufi,
   placing words in the mouth
   of god, says:

   when my servant draws near to me
   through obligatory and free devotion

   I become the hearing with which he hears
   the seeing with which he sees

   the hands with which he touches
   the feet with which he walks

These words are spoken
   by an inconceivable being,
   a being that cannot be confined.

The Sufi is not seeing, not hearing—
   his perceptions
   are impersonal perceptions.

His limited self
   is giving way
   to an unfathomable god.

We find
   something similar
   in the Buddhist tradition.

A Brahmin crosses India from the sea
   to the country's center to seek teachings
   from the Buddha—

in a nutshell,
   the Buddha says:

> *In seeing, just seeing; in hearing, just hearing;*
> *in tasting, just tasting; in smelling, just smelling;*
> *in feeling, just feeling; in thinking, just thinking.*

It was enough for the Brahmin,
   who awakened.

But what does
   just mean?

It means the elimination
   of the reality of a tangible subject
   and tangible object;

it leaves seeing whole.
   A seeing in which the totality
   of my being participates.

A seeing beyond any notion
   of inside and outside.

A seeing without a seer;
   a seeing without anything seen.

It leaves intimacy,
   an intimacy leaving only presence,
   only awareness.

How is *I*-less seeing,
   I-less hearing
   possible?

When wind blows,
   do we look for a blower
   apart from the blowing?

When fire burns,
   do we look for a burner
   apart from the fire?

Can't I see the way the wind blows
   and feel the way fire burns when I lie
   on the floor with my eyes closed?

Is there any rester apart from the resting?
   Is there any feeler separated
   from feeling bodily sensations?

The sense of being at rest
   on the floor
   or on one's back

creates separation,
   creates duality.
   Is the notion of floor,

or the notion of back, anything but
   imagination, a construct based
   on the sensation of hardness, of coldness?

A construct useful if
   we're to clean the floor, useful
   if we need to protect our back,

but it misleads
   if we're concerned with intimacy,
   with full presence.

Can I rest on the floor
   like the fire burns?

Can I walk
   like the wind blows?

can you stand

you may walk

for half an hour

does it make sense

how long can we walk for
at each instant

just be walking
can you walk faster

faster with respect to what

can we walk at two different
speeds at the same time

just walk fast

you may stop

just be standing
you may let your eyes close

place one hand on your forehead
one hand on your lower back

move very slightly the upper part
of your body forward

and backward

forward

backward

now sideways

to the left
to the right

you may stop

just be standing

raise your hands
cover your eyes
with your hands

are you trying to see

just be standing
with covered eyes

slowly you may let
your hands come down until

they are at rest

now you may discover the visual field
by opening your eyes

it doesn't matter what you see
what does matter is
that you are seeing

imagine some one blind for months
who suddenly discovers
seeing

the simple experience
of seeing

you may make a team of two persons

one in front of the other
facing the same direction

the one in back may place hands
on the shoulders of the person in front

the person in back
may close both eyes

slowly you may walk
together

trusting or not trusting
the person in front

nothing to transform

just walk together

you may stop

switch position
the person in back placing hands
on the shoulders of the person in front

the person in front closing eyes

you may walk

the person in the back guides
the person in front

leading by small indications
given by the hands

you may stop

you may open your eyes

and discover seeing

close your eyes
and walk together

you may stop

open your eyes and discover
what seeing is

not what you see

but the mere fact of seeing

does seeing happen
anywhere

you may walk alone

NOW HERE NOWHERE

Desire to transform anything
   relies on a comparison between
   what is happening

and what could happen.
   It implies distance between
   oneself and experience.

The need to change anything
   arises from dissatisfaction,
   from fragmentation

created by the distance
   between two instances
   of oneself.

The wish to improve
   anything is to wish
   for wholeness,

though one is seldom
   conscious of this.

Desire to transform
   anything sustains the gap
   one tries to fill.

It perpetuates distance;
   it puts one in an impossible
   situation.

It is as if one were trying
   to open an already
   open door:

the door of wholeness
   already and always open.

Water cannot
   brake a stream.
   Only an element

outside the flow
   can stop it—
   a fallen tree.

When we set out
   to transform experience,
   we place ourselves

outside experience
   to judge and control it.
   Without this split,

an experience cannot
   be judged as there is nothing
   outside it

to measure it,
   no yardstick. Hence
   any transformation,

any wish for improvement,
   is incompatible
   with completeness.

We spend
   our lives transforming
   our situation.

We may even find
   improvement,
      yet this is at great cost.

For little benefit
   we sacrifice the totality
   of our being.

When we are the experience,
   who or what can wish
   for transformation?

Is there anything else?
   There is only the simplicity
   of the experience itself

when there is no distinction
   between the one who experiences
   and that which is experienced.

There is only
   the simplicity
   of the experience itself

when there is no distinction
   between the seeker
   and that which is sought.

And when there is only the simplicity
   of the experience itself,
      where is duality?

Where is fragmentation?
   Who or what is left unfulfilled?

Let's explore this.
   Let's try.

Grasp your left hand
   with your left hand.
   Can you do that?

Grasping your left hand
   with the right is easy;
   they're separate.

But a left hand
   trying to grasp itself
   is senseless.

It would mean
   a left hand separate
   from itself.

Try to grasp your left hand with
   your left hand—don't
   give up too quickly.

Don't be too
   easily convinced.

Try to grasp your right hand with
   your right hand.
   Is that easier?

Be careful. If you believe
   you can do it by closing
   your hand tightly,

which hand is grasped?
   And which hand
   is grasping?

Nothing
   to improve.

If I wanted
   something else,
   something other

than what is
   happening now,

I'd be separating
   the what should be
   from what is.

But if I rest
   in just that,

in the simplicity
   of the wanting, there is
   no gap, no time.

In the search
   for something,
   if we just rest in the seeking

duality will not be
   sustained.

Nothing
   to improve.

We may grasp
   at models of effortlessness,
   aimlessness,

we may want our way
   of experiencing to conform
   with such models,

but again, this creates duality
   between the what should be
   and what is.

At no time do we need to change,
    to transform, to keep
    anything.

Rest simply, rather,
    in whatever
    we do.

When we pretend
    to do something
    other,

other than what
    we are doing,
    we are fragmented.

Nothing
    to transform.

No model adheres,
    not even
    a beautiful one.

Effortlessness,
    aimlessness—
    let's just do whatever it is

we are doing.
    Not making
    duality,

duality between
    one who rests and
    resting place.

Someone resting
    in a resting place implies
    duality, limitation.

Nothing
to change.

Are we present
in what we do
at every instant?

Or are we doing
the not-yet-here,
that which we are wishing for?

In the simplicity
of the experience,

is the doing of what we do
happening
anywhere?

The action is
not located anywhere.

In order for something
to be placed somewhere there needs
to be at least two phenomena.

When there is only one,
there is nothing with respect to
where it may be located.

Bodily sensations
are not in the body—

for the sensations themselves,
the sensations are not happening
anywhere.

From the left hand's point of view,
it is not located anywhere.
It is nowhere.

Nothing
    to improve.

If there were only one universe
    and therefore nothing
    outside it,

could we locate the universe?
    Here without any possibility
    of *there* is devoid of signification.

Here nondualistically
    is meaningless.

Now here
    nowhere.

you may stand

just being standing

can you take a first step

where is it now

now you are standing
just standing

can you take
a second step

what does second mean
when one takes a step

a previous step
does not exist anymore

how could we ever
take another step

another step
with respect to what

past steps do not exist
future steps do not exist
another step does not exist

first second keep the sense
of duration

of time

can you walk
going nowhere

walk fast

going nowhere

SACRED SPACE

We carry our training for the world;
   we gather causes
   to bring the effects we want.

And we can be skillful finding
   solutions to the problems
   the world presents.

But our attitude
   may need to be different when
   we're concerned with the essential.

The essential,
   which doesn't depend on time,
   and is already here.

When the object of our quest is already
   here a new attitude
   may be required from us.

In the Buddhist Literature
   there's the story of Angulimala,

who believed if he killed a thousand men
   he'd become free.

By the time he'd already killed 999,
   nearby villagers went to the Buddha
   to seek help.

Soon after, in the forest one day,
   the Buddha heard someone shouting.
   It was Angulimala.

"Stop! Stop! Why are you running so fast!"
Angulimala shouted, but
the Buddha was walking peacefully.

It was Angulimala himself who
was running. And so the Buddha said,
"You're the one who's running, not me."

At hearing this, Angulimala was able
to finally stop, and as the Buddha
spoke to him he became enlightened.

I like this image of a fast running man unable
to catch up with the Buddha
peacefully walking along,

the man shouting, Stop! But the Buddha
had stopped the moment
he awoke.

How often do we stop in our lives?
Have we ever met anyone
who has truly stopped?

Of course, to stop doesn't
mean that one becomes motionless.

To stop is to stop looking
for what is already here,
to stop subjecting the present to a future aim.

Cultivating bondage is no way to freedom.
To find what is already here requires
a new way of exploring.

Sometimes I ask
simple questions that lead
to simple answers,

and complex questions
    that lead to complex answers,
    but I prefer to ask

impossible questions
    that lead
    to no answers.

Sometimes I see the work
    as a koan
    in which the situation

is the question,
    a situation which doesn't allow
    any answer to arise.

We've questioned the notion
    of time. Let's question
    the notion of place.

We may roughly understand our practice
    as resting in the present,
    but we may wonder in what place.

What is the proper place
    in which to be?

When I was in Israel,
    in Tel Aviv, I was impressed
    by all the tourists.

Groups of tourists
    wearing badges
    with names like *Quest Tour*.

They were pilgrims who had traveled
    far to reach specific places
    in the holy land.

The tradition of pilgrimage
    is an old one.

Meditators in Syria
    by the fifth century were troubled
    by all the Greek tourists.

Traveling to Jerusalem to Mecca
    to Varanasi to Ife in Africa
    can take a long time.

It can take a long time to reach
    the aim of a journey
    and of a life.

In the Muslim tradition, pilgrimage
    is so important some people
    save up their entire lives for it.

The aim of the journey for a pilgrim
    is the place, the place most
    meaningful to be.

A place from which there is no
    departure,
    nowhere else to go.

Mircea Eliade described it
    as the most dense place
    of being, of presence.

The sacred place is
    the center around which
    the world is organized.

North, south, east, and west—
    the world is seen
    according to this light.

And if you go away from it
   into the unknown, into darkness,
   you enter chaos.

Far from the center, chaos is where
   barbarians live, and demons,
   and whatever is feared.

The most dense place of being
   is the center.

At the foot of Mount Kailash
   along with a few friends I met Hindu
   pilgrims making offerings.

They invited us to stay
   for prayers. They were so moved
   they had tears in their eyes.

Pointing, they said, "Look at Lord Shiva."
   The mountain itself is the Lord
   for these pilgrims.

"Now we can die," they said. "As for you,
   make any wish and it will be granted
   as you are here with Lord Shiva."

Mount Kailash
   was the end of all possible
   journeys for them.

Where is our place,
   we may wonder.
   Where is the place for us to be?

Let's not consider outer pilgrimage,
   but an inner pilgrimage,
   our meditation.

Should we look within ourselves
    for a specific place?
    Is the most dense place of being

in the head, or in the heart?
    Or is that place in the abdomen,
    which some of us call

by that strange name, *hara*.
    Where is the most dense place of being
    from which there's nowhere else to go?

In some yogic traditions,
    there are subtle descriptions
    of the inner journey.

Mandalas, in the Tibetan tradition,
    are complex maps
    that can illustrate what's inside.

It's important to discover
    where this place is:
    the most dense place of being.

The profane
    is opposite the sacred.

Profane means to be in front
    of the temple
    and not inside it.

In our inner pilgrimage,
    are we in the sacred place?
    In the profane place?

Can the most dense place
    of presence be outside
    the searcher?

Can the most dense place
    of presence be found in the head
    or heart or wherever else?

Is the place with the densest sense of being
    right in the experience itself?

Is the place with the densest sense of being
    right in bodily sensation
    when there is bodily sensation?

Right in the experience itself:
    in a thought
    when there is a thought?

What if we bring our attention,
    our awareness, to a specific place,
    any specific place, any part of the body?

If we try as meditators to bring
    our awareness to our walking we'll be
    in the profane place in front of the temple.

When we bring our attention somewhere
    we're in the profane world.

Bringing our awareness
    to any experience means we're not
    in the most dense place of existence.

We don't need to bring our awareness anywhere—
    awareness is always within the arising
    of the experience itself.

We don't need to make any separation
    between bodily sensations and awareness.
    Bodily sensations are already awareness.

Thought is already awareness.
　We don't need to bring
　awareness to the thought.

What we're exploring
　is not the body
　but the body's awareness.

We're just exploring
　the body of awareness.

We may wonder where
　the body's awareness is,
　imagining it's in the body,

but the body's awareness will only be
　in the body if we stand outside ourselves
　trying to figure out where it is.

The center gives orientation.
　It's not located anywhere.

The experience of the body's awareness
　or the thought's awareness is not located anywhere
　from the standpoint of the experience.

There is nothing outside
　the experience of the body's awareness.

Awareness is not located anywhere.
　It is not situated in space,

for space would then be something known by
　experience: it's not a characteristic
　of awareness itself.

In our exploration
　it's not necessary to direct
　our awareness.

Rather, let awareness
    play out on its own.

Rest simply with experiences,
    with bodily sensations,
    thoughts.

If one tries to bring awareness
    someplace then one may not
    be complete.

And so now you know
    where the place to be is.

let's explore this

would you like to stand

*can you place one hand
on your forehead*

*you may place the other
on your abdomen*

just be standing

*you may withdraw
both hands*

*bring them to a position of rest
by your thighs*

*just standing
nothing else*

*when one is
just standing*

is one standing anywhere

anywhere
with respect to what

you may make a team
of three people

one will stand in the middle
the others
will stand on either side

the other two will each move
the arms and shoulders of the
middle person upward
parallel to the body

just be standing in
this position

you may bring the arms
down slowly

just be standing

you may walk

place one hand on your head
walk

just be walking with
one hand on your head

some may think
it's silly

to be walking with
one's hand on one's head

meaningfulness
or meaninglessness
are just concepts
that take us away from
the experience

is the need for meaning
bondage

when you walk
by the door you may take
one of the numerous shoes there

you may walk carrying
one shoe

just be walking
with one shoe in your hand

walking as slowly or
as fast as you like

walk

we walk like this
not for the shoes
not for us

but to question our need
for meaning

if we look for
meaning in everything
we're concerned with meaning
not with experiences
not with life

just be walking
with the shoe in hand

you may leave the shoes by the door

make teams of
two persons

you may sit facing each other
your hands resting on your knees

one person takes the hand
of the other and turns it slowly
palm upward

let it rest

turn the palm
downward

let it rest

turn the palm
upward

let it rest

place the hand carefully
on the knee of the other person

you may stand
find a place to rest on the floor
on your back

place one hand
on your chest

withdraw your hand
bring it to the floor

ATOPIC ACHRONIC

Strange, maybe,
  to consider literature
  when our subject is meditation.

And yet I wish to address
  this subject of literature,
  of writers.

Writers so aware of the power
  of words that they seek to free
  themselves from them.

What a hard situation!
  Having only words to destroy
  the power of words.

Only a language, George Bataille said,
  that works toward its own annihilation
  doesn't reify reality;

only a language that destroys
  itself as it is expressed
  isn't misleading.

I read a slender novel,
  Le Dernier Homme, by Maurice Blanchot,
  and I didn't understand a thing!

Two words from the Greek describe it:
  achronic, meaning "no time,"
  and *atopic*, meaning "no place."

Such fiction, it can be said,
    isn't happening
    in any time, or in any place,

nor is there any character
    to whom things happen.

Blanchot skillfully made fiction
    without time, or place,
    or character, or event.

A writer knows the power of language—
    how words give us something
    to grasp, and to believe in.

The phrase *the marquise*
    went out at five o'clock for tea
    gives us something to believe in:

someone going somewhere at such
    and such a time. We believe it.
    This is the power of words.

Bataille, Blanchot, Beckett,
    and others may use language, however,
    to ruin such belief.

These two words: *achronic* and *atopic*—
    no time and no place—
    directly concern our exploration.

In spiritual circles, workshops, talks, and retreats
    words like *here* and *now* are used like mantras,
    as if they express truth.

Don't the words *here* and *now*
    depend on place, on time—
    on *before* and *after?*

Don't they express dualism?
   Don't the words *here* and *now*
   express a fragmented understanding?

We may find this notion that things
   don't happen in place or time
   more challenging.

An experience happens somewhere only when
   we place ourselves outside the experience
   as an observer, as an experiencer.

An experience happens
   somewhere only with respect to
   another somewhere.

When we are the experience itself,
   can it be experienced
   at any place?

When we bring our attention
   somewhere, don't we create a place?

When I move my attention to my arm,
   mindful of sensations in my arm,
   am I not making a place, a world?

Isn't this how we structure
   our daily lives, our reality?

This structure of our lives,
   our reality, is exactly
   what we're questioning.

We're questioning the way we create
   a world through attitude and language
   and purposeful mindfulness.

When we believe in the world
   in which we live,
   when we believe in separation,

when we believe in duality,
  in subject and object, we're creating
  our cage, our prison, our chains.

Or we may keep on creating the world,
  while yet realizing the fictional
  aspect of our creation.

Though they may sound harsh,
  these two words—achronic and atopic—
  illuminate with their precision.

No time, no place,
  no when, no where.

In order to explore this,
  we may have to stop following
  our tendency to be an observer,

our tendency to observe
  our experiences, our thoughts.

If we set ourselves up as an observer
  of our thoughts we could locate them
  with respect to this observer.

If we are just thoughts—if we are
  the arising thoughts—where could
  we locate them, and with respect to what?

Can we say a thought is *here*, or *there?*
  Here or *there*
  is the thought that we are

when *here* arises with the simultaneous
  impossibility of *there*—
  it has no meaning.

This may be said to be true
  for all experiences.

Tasting, thinking, smelling, hearing,
    tactile sensation, seeing—

the simplicity of our experiences—
    where do they happen?

The seeing itself, and not the object—
    where does seeing happen?

Can we say it's happening in front of us,
    or behind us, or inside, or outside,
    and with respect to what?

We may inquire of all our senses
    in this way without building
    any sense of location.

Can I just walk, just experience
    bodily sensations, and not
    invent stories?

If there is nothing other than bodily
    sensations, in which space could I move?
    Toward what, away from what?

In our work, we don't need to cultivate
    the attempt to be mindful
    of something specific.

Just walking, just seeing,
    just hearing—we don't need to
    try to walk or see or hear.

Maybe we're as absent as
    the characters in Blanchot's novel:
    we are nowhere.

Yet that is
    to be questioned.

can you stand

you may walk

you may make teams of three

one person will sit
on the floor

one person will be
behind

another in front

the person behind will place
hands on the shoulders of
the person seated

the person in front will place
hands on the knees of
the person seated

just be seated
not trying to accomplish
anything

just a way of being together

you may withdraw
your hands

you may stand

you may walk

when you meet another person you may place
your hand on his or her shoulder
and you may walk
together

now the person behind will
take a small sandbag
from the basket and

place it on the person
walking in front

you may dissolve the teams

those with no sandbags
may go to get one

you may stop

I speak of no aim and
I ask you to go and get a sandbag

sometimes I know what we will do with it
I have an aim

now I ask you to take
a sandbag

I don't know what
we will do with it

so I have no aim and
you have a sandbag
on your head

you may walk

can you feel the weight of the sandbag

in your neck

in your chest

in your breath

you may stop

you may rest on the floor

NAGARJUNA

To discover
   the truth of the world
   one doesn't need—

one doesn't need
   to question the far away.

Remote planets,
   the split second after
   the birth of the universe—

to question the far away
   may not lead to
   great discoveries.

Knowledge may be extended,
   more information gathered,
   but our understanding will not deepen.

Questioning that
   which is close,
   closest to us—

questioning that which is
   so close it seems impossible
   to question it—

may prove to be
   just what requires
   challenge.

Some people have the rare
    passion to doubt
    what others assume to be true.

In Greece, five centuries before Christ,
    Zeno questioned
    the unquestionable—

movement.
    He found it was impossible.

Plato, Aristotle, all the great
    philosophers after Zeno
    fought to dismiss his findings,

but their dismissal
    wasn't conclusive,
    and some philosophers continue

continue to try to find errors in Zeno's negation
    of such common experiences
    as motion.

If we take seeming evidence as truth—
    the sun setting, for example,
    over the horizon—

such evidence would prove the fallacy
    of Copernicus' vision that the earth
    turns around the sun.

Contemplating
    the reality of movement,
    Zeno thought

that as long as anything is
    in a space equal to itself,
    it is at rest.

In every instant
    of its flight, for example, an arrow
    is in a space equal to itself,

the flying arrow
    at rest in every instant.

But if the arrow is at rest,
    we may wonder
    how it can move.

When we wonder whether we can be
    in two places at the same time,
    are we not questioning movement in a similar way?

In the Buddhist tradition,
    Nagarjuna also said
    that movement is illusory.

He wondered
    where movement starts:

Does it start in stillness?
    Does it start in movement?

If movement starts in stillness,
    how can something be said
    to move?

If something starts in movement,
    it has been ever moving,
    and never started.

Nagarjuna shows
    that any point of view
    leads to absurd consequences.

Any statement contains
    its own contradiction.

Nagarjuna rejects
affirmation and negation.

He doesn't teach
that nothing exists,
but rather to take things lightly.

Things taken lightly
are like a dream,
an illusion.

When taken seriously
things are as hard
as concrete.

Not grasping
at the world,
taking things lightly,

flowing with the illusory
movement of things,
dancing their dreamlike dance,

the world itself not seen
as existing,
as not existing—

Nagarjuna's philosophy
follows the texts
of the *Prajnaparamita*.

Texts about emptiness
and form,
form and emptiness.

In trying to find anything
real in the form that appears,
one is left with nothing,

yet this nothing
   allows form to appear,
   the flowers to blossom.

The dreamlike can play,
   interact,
   gather together and separate.

Real things,
   concrete things, are forever isolated
   in their own being—

isolated,
   unable to step out
   of their own self-reliance,

unable to know or to be known,
   to cause
   or to be caused—

let's explore
   the reality of movement.

We can't say
   we will take Nagarjuna's point of view,
   as he has none,

but maybe we will question
   with the same spirit.

Question what
   Nagarjuna questioned.

Question in our own way
   while walking, while standing still,
   while about to walk.

What really happens
   as we take a step?

can you stand

let your eyes close

you may lift your shoulders
being standing
shoulders lifted

let the right shoulder down slowly
let the left shoulder down slowly

place one hand on your head
feel the hand rising

sense the way
you are being standing

you may withdraw
your hand
let it come down by your side

as you open your eyes
can you feel the weight
of your eyelids

discover the visual field

just standing
just seeing

you may take one step forward

take another

you know there is no other

take a step forward

and walk

and stop

do stopping
and walking exist
at the same time

if not
what could connect them

can we walk and be still at the same time

now we are
motionless

when movement and stillness
exist at the same time

what kind of movement
is such that it can be still

is it anything but
the appearance of movement

let's explore

how does movement start
let's inquire into the very beginning

does it start in movement

now you are still
do you have to wait to move
to start to move

movement would precede movement

movement would start
before movement started

does movement
start in stillness

how could stillness ever move

you may walk
just walk

don't bother about its beginning
just being walking

it seems to be happening

we're walking

let's question the happening

just experience the body
of sensations

not the body as a visual form
for some outsider

not an imaginary body
for an insider
for our imagination

just the body of sensations
as it's experienced
simply

while walking let the body
of sensations experience

the body of sensation

let's not step out
from the conscious body
from ourselves

is the sensation
happening anywhere

for the sensation
the body of sensation
is not located anywhere

in its simplicity

located
with respect to what

where there is no location
how can there be any movement

with no
where

can there be stillness

let's investigate

just be walking

let the body of sensation
experience the body of sensation

let the body of awareness
be aware
nothing else

if we're not locating ourselves
by building a space between
between me
and the world

if we're not looking at the walls
not creating the opposition
between here and there

when the body of awareness is all there is

in the impossibility of anything
outside

can anything move

can anything be still

you may walk

you may stop

does it make a difference

HOPI

Points of view,
   beliefs,
   can be questioned,

but can reality
   be questioned?

Can the reality
   of our ordinary world
   be dependent

on our way of thinking?
   Philosophers in their frenzy
   will question anything.

Their obscure talk.
   The contradictions so smoothly
   and intelligently explained

may leave us in confusion.
   Wouldn't it be better
   to stay away from philosophers,

from Zeno and Nagarjuna?
   Wouldn't it be better to rely on
   the down to earth,

like the Hopi in Arizona?
   They don't waste time writing
   about the world.

They live in it.
  They live in the concrete world,
  growing corn, beans,

cotton, and tobacco.
  They hunt deer, antelope,
  and elk.

They live in
  the palpable world,
  building solid houses

of sandstone and adobe
  with roof beams hewn of
  pine and juniper.

They live in
  the concrete world,
  as we do.

But is it exactly
  the same world?
  We're not questioning

their mythology,
  their cosmology.
  We're questioning

the world of common
  activity—walking, carrying water,
  counting the days.

Is it the world we know?
  The world we know is a vast
  homogenous timeless space

through which flows
  the continuum of time.

According to Benjamin Lee Worf,
   an American anthropologist,
   it is another world for the Hopi.

A world not contained
   within a stable space
   in which time does not move.

The scholar noted that
   there are no words in the Hopi language
   for *past, present,* or *future.*

No notion of a purely
   independent space.

Something happening,
   for instance, in a distant village
   is not considered as happening

at the same time.
   It can only be known later.

And yet the language
   of the Hopi
   lacks nothing.

It expresses the world
   as well and as precisely
   as other languages,

but instead of
   wielding notions
   of time and space

the Hopi speak
   of the manifested
   and manifesting.

This understanding
   of the Hopi language may not
   be exact. But it opens

our reflection
  on the nature of language.

Language is built
  on convention; it is relative.
  Although we might not

phrase it so bluntly, let us ask
  ourselves whether we are
  free of the confusion

we may witness
  in children—the confusion
  of name with object.

The difference
  between the name
  and the object it refers to

isn't clear for children.
  The name is part
  of the thing.

Sometimes, children write
  the name of an object below
  a drawing of it.

The name belongs to
  the thing—to the sun, for example,
  because it is yellow.

The object, for children,
  naturally seems to possess
  its name.

Parents spend hours
  naming things
  to their children.

Names seem an essential aspect
   of the things themselves.
   The name *stone*

seems heavier
   than the name *feather*.
   The name seems

to naturally possess
   the qualities of its object.

Our guard is up, though.
   Certainly, we wouldn't say
   one name is heavier than another.

But isn't the mental image of a friend
   more friendly than the mental image
   of an indifferent person?

We are fascinated
   by our thoughts.

When desire or hatred arises
   in our mind don't we confuse image
   with object or person?

And if not, why does
   desire or hatred arise
   dependent on the image?

We confuse thoughts
   for what they point to—the thought
   of a glass of water isn't wet;

the thought of one's beloved
   is not the beloved.

Why would happiness
   or sadness arise when thinking
   about a person?

In the Hopi language,
  there is no plural for day,
  year, or even minute.

For the Hopi, the notion
  of day is of a different kind
  than one made of objects.

How to add up
  the days? How many days
  can we have all at once?

To have three days, we need
  three days. And yet on the first day
  we have only that, the first day.

On the third day
  we have only that,
  the third day.

The Hopi say
  it isn't possible to take
  ten steps.

When taking one step
  the next does not
  yet exist.

And where does
  the first step go when
  the second step is taken?

Notions of days, and steps,
  of present, future, and past
  are just mental images.

They are useful
  in a fragmented world.

But to discover a deeper truth
we have to stop clinging
to concepts.

Concepts bring efficiency,
not wholeness. Concepts
bring knowledge, not truth.

Is it possible
to experience the world

outside the notion
of space and time?
What could that mean?

you may stand up
you may make teams of two persons

face each other

one person will raise arms
forward to shoulder height
and lift palms up

the other person will bring hands
up to the hands of the other person

feel the contact
respect whatever you feel

at ease
or not at ease

The first person
moves the hands
up or down

to the left or to the right
the hands of two persons
moving together

the first person is the one
who moves the hands

you may stop

bring your hands
to rest

in their natural position

EXILE

We are
  in exile.

To be in exile is to be out
  of the present.

Even trying to return
  from exile to be present
  is to be in exile.

Seeking the Promised Land
  implies one isn't
  in it already.

Seeking the Promised Land
  is to be in exile.

This Promised Land
  keeps us out
  by luring us into the future.

When we are the object
  of our own quest we are not
  where we are.

The wish to find ourselves
  is to be

not where we are.
  To be not where we are
  is to be in exile.

To be in exile is not
　　so much to be in another place,
　　another world,

rather, it is to be out
　　of the world,
　　out of reality.

But it's not as though
　　we're in a foreign land:

we are in exile
　　in our own land,
　　our own home.

How could we be
　　not where we are?

How could we ever be
　　out of the present?

We are not aware
　　of where we are—

we are presently
　　not present.

What is this place of exile
　　where our homeland is obscured?
　　What hides it?

Time confines us within
　　a world of shallowness.

A world of shallowness
　　made of imagination
　　and concepts.

Time veils our homeland
　　disguising it
　　as a foreign place.

So long as we're in time,
    we are in exile.

To move from
    the foreign to the promised
    we need to do,

to gather the necessary conditions,
    clear away obstacles,
    get organized.

In gathering the necessary
    conditions we need to be
    in charge, in control,

and to control we need
    to be outside,
    at a distance from something.

Only an element outside
    the flow—a fallen tree—
    can stop a stream.

Control is
    our exile.

How to bridge,
    if it is even possible,
    this distance?

The Buddha once said
    to his disciples it's impossible
    to travel to the end of the world.

And then he said that without traveling
    to the end of the world
    emancipation is impossible.

He then withdrew into the forest
  leaving his disciples
  perplexed.

We could say
  it's impossible to travel
  to the Promised Land—

a future Promised Land
  is nothing but a dream.

Yet outside the Promised Land
  in unawareness
  there is no peace.

What needs to change,
  be transformed,
  for our exile to be over?

To attempt to transform
  is to be at distance—

to be split between
  transformer
  and the transformed.

Transformation
  is our exile.

Transformation
  at a distance
  is transformation accomplished

from the point of view
  of distance.

It is transformation accomplished
  from the point of view
  of another.

Transforming emotions,
   thoughts, from a distance
   is just an exchange

of constraint, not
   authentic
   transformation.

True transformation arises of itself,
   without any notion
   of aim and improvement;

true transformation happens in the absence
   of time when the meditator
   is simply the experience.

It happens when emotions, thoughts,
   are experienced without any distance,
   in oneness.

Emotions, thoughts
   find their own balance in oneness
   and are naturally free.

True transformation
   happens when there is no time
   for anything to happen.

It happens when
   there is no time for anything
   to be preserved.

It happens when
   there is no time.

How to bridge this gap
   between subject
   and object?

How to bridge this gap
   between the action
   and the aim of the action;

how to bridge this gap
   between the observer and
   the observed?

When the observing mind drops
   its objective,
   there's no observer

and no observed,
   there is just observing.
   When we point

at a bird on a tree
   with our finger, we're not
   concerned with our finger,

but with a bird.
   When a dancer
   stretches her hand

she is present
   with it; she's not preoccupied
   with something else, the backdrop.

Can we observe
   as the dancer dances,
   without orientation?

In just observing
   there is just
   simply presence.

A presence
   without anyone.

When the action
    not subject to aim rests
    in itself, where is separation?

In wholly doing something—
    acting totally in oneness—
    there's no aim, no result,

no *I*, no actor,
    only act.

For the fire in all
    its burning there's no aim,
    no choice.

To have a choice
    there must be two,
    two of something.

When there is two of something
    there is distance
    between one and the other.

To have a choice
    is to be at a distance.
    In choice is our exile.

If the great way
    is not difficult for those
    who have no preferences,

the way has ended
    for those who abide
    without choice.

In the absence of distance—
    in awareness—
    where is the other?

In awareness,
  where is choice?

In the fullness of presence,
  there is no exile
  as there is nothing else.

In awareness,
  there is no homeland
  as there is nothing foreign.

As there is no choice
  there is no freedom.

As there is no choice
  there is no bondage—
  there is just it.

It without
  the possibility of not it—without any distance,
  is ungraspable.

can you stand

walk

you may stop

you may make teams
of three persons

two persons will be
seated
on either side
of the one standing

when the person
in the middle
is ready
that person will
signal

the others will place
one hand on the knee

of the one standing

you may be simply
physically aware

nothing to transform

nothing to improve

can you feel
at ease

or
not at ease

nothing to change

nothing to keep

you may withdraw
your hands

you may walk

slowly

fast

as you like

walking

when walking
is there any distance
between yourself
and the floor

just walk

is there any distance

between yourself
and the floor

you may stop

just be

standing

standing on the floor

or just standing

is standing happening

anywhere

you may walk

slowly

fast
walking

you may just walk

TRACES

Memories:
    I took a train from
    New Jersey to New York.

People were reading
    magazines, newspapers,
    novels.

Mornings, when I'm
    in Geneva, on the bus,
    I meet with people

going to work.
    What a boring trip,
    for some.

Occasionally they
    fall asleep, trying
    to resume their dreams.

There are those
    who read, preferring
    to spend time

with fictitious
    characters rather than
    with the other

bored people, the
    half-asleep,
    the dreaming.

These travelers
  may pass a lot of time
  everyday

in nonexistent places,
  with nonexistent
  people.

However accurate
  a writer's description
  of a place,

it will always be
  a mere description,
  nothing else.

Does a real place
  exist in the morning
  or does it exist in the evening?

These travelers
  are in a dream,
  the dream of another person.

They know it is
  fiction, they know
  nothing is true, and yet

they lose themselves
  in it. That is what they want.

Some writers use
  their own name to make
  stories appear real.

They describe
  their life; they may
  pen an autobiography.

They imagine they're writing
  themselves closer to reality,
  not fiction.

They proffer events
  large and small; they proffer
  the details of their life.

Discoveries, difficulties,
  successes, failures—they tell us
  their story.

When a writer describes
  her life as a child or as a teenager—
  that life is no more.

When a writer describes
  a house she once lived in, that house
  may no longer be standing.

Is that life, that house
  any different from fiction?

The sources may
  be different. Fiction is drawn
  from the imagination;

an autobiography is drawn
  from memories. But their nature is
  the same: dream-like images.

Not to exist anymore or not
  to exist at all—
  is there a difference?

Reading a novel or a biography
  on the train projects us into another time
  in another place; it keeps us in a fiction.

Some people keep
    a writing journal and mark it
    everyday.

Reading it may help
    them to keep in touch with
    the real world.

But at what time
    does the writer write?

Does he write
    in the morning, or does he
    write in the evening?

He doesn't write
    of the events as they happen,
    in any case.

But even if he were
    to write of things as they are
    right then,

in that moment—
    writing of the temperature of the paper,
    for instance, or of the lightness

or heaviness of the pen, the curve
    of his body as he writes; writing
    of the light in the room,

and of the joy he feels,
    or is it sadness, or yearning—
    not writing of the past, of what was,

and not imagining events,
    but just writing of what is
    happening now,

just describing, and yet,
  to describe a thing isn't
  the thing itself.

Likewise
  with judging people.

What if I were to judge people
  on the New Jersey train:
  Is that a nice hat?

And,
  *Is that a nice coat
  she's wearing?*

But what is the color
  of a nice hat, anyway?
  And of a nice coat?

*The train is slow; the train
  is late.* Or is it too fast?

If I think the train is late,
  it means
  I live in time:

One may try to find time,
  not recognizing that it is nothing
  but a fiction.

In his *Confessions*, Saint Augustine,
  the great Christian theologian,
  spoke of time's disarray,

its elusiveness, its intangible nature.
  What is time? he asked. And who can explain it?
  So long as no one asks me, he said,

so long as I don't have to explain it,
   I know. But if I try to explain it,
   I don't know.

The past
   no longer exists. As for the future,
   it does not yet exist.

And as for the present—
   how can we even say it exists?

We can find
   such questioning in the tradition
   of Mahayana Buddhism.

If we look into the mind
   we discover that past thoughts
   don't exist anymore.

Future thoughts
   have yet to be born.

How can there be
   a present thought
   in the middle of nowhere?

Time exists only in the world
   of language, in stories
   and legends.

Time is not to be found
   in the absence of thoughts.

In the absence of thoughts,
   nothing can be kept.
   Nothing endures.

To gaze once more on the sun
   as it rose this morning, to hear the birds
   clattering again in that light,

to feel the cool breeze
    as I opened the door last night—it's
    all impossible.

I can try to keep an experience, try
    to make it last:
    an impossible task.

The light in the sky
    is changing; the breeze has stopped.

As experiences are ungraspable,
    we grasp at mental images.

Mental images that we confuse
    for experiences.

Mental images are traces—
    traces, habitual patterns.

As we need to rest
    on something which seems stable,
    firm, we cling to traces.

On the traceless, therefore
    timeless,
    we project the notion of time and duration.

To find comfort and security
    we make something
    out of an ungraspable reality.

We grasp so quickly,
    conceptualize so conditionally,
    that we're never aware of the traceless.

Holding to an experience by means of a concept,
    I solidify it:
    I make it into something,

a something
   that can be opposed
   to another something.

In a similar way,
   I hold on to the notion
   of a subject.

On the impersonal world of experiences,
   with a single letter, *I*—
   I trace a person,

as if creating
   a blower of the wind,
   a rainer of the rain.

A single letter
   sets two worlds apart:

the world of object
   and the world of subject,
   and thus comes exile.

We are all storytellers.
   We spin the fiction of our lives,
   the fiction that we are.

I may move
   my hand in a way that one
   could call circular—

but there is no circle.
   Can my hand be
   at more than one place at a time?

If so,
   where is the circle?

One is holding only traces, memories:
    it is through such traces that one speaks
    of movement, and of a circle.

The fiction that *I am*
    is created in a similar way.

Holding to traces of past moments,
    holding to imagined future moments,
    I draw an enduring character, *I*.

But just as with the circle
    seen in the movement of a hand,
    I am no where to be found.

Once I've created the main character, *I*—
    once I've put distance between
    myself and experience—

my story can't be but a story of exile,
    of a hopeless wandering.

Exile can end only with the end
    of the split between
    object and subject;

exile can end only if the fictitious nature
    of object and subject
    is seen through.

As the main character
    is also the storyteller,
    he resists his own ending.

The world of traces, of fiction,
    isn't another world

as there is no real world
    with respect to which it could be
    other.

The memory of the circle
   drawn by my hand is only
   the trace of a trace,

the trace of something that
   never was.

We don't need to read fiction
   to be in a dream-like reality

as there is no real world
   behind the dream,
   behind the traces.

There is a difference between the fiction
   found in books
   and the reality of our everyday life.

The fiction found in a book
   depends solely on the writer
   and on the reader's imagination.

We live in an illusory world,
   an illusory world
   that we share,

an illusion kept alive
   by tacit convention.

The reality of our everyday life
   depends on shared
   conditionality—

it is a common dream,
   not a private one.

Can you move your hand
   in a circular way, not holding on
   to traces;

can you move your hand
   and not be drawn in by the notion
   of a circle? Let's explore.

Know when you are dealing
   with traces.

Know when you are just
   experiencing.

you may walk

stop

can you feel the way you stand

move your hand
in a circular way

are you keeping a trace
in mind

is there any circle

or just a hand at one place
at a time

are you just a body
of presence

are you in a mere mental world
of images

you may stop

let your hand rest naturally
along your thigh

just be standing

you may move your hand
from left to right

from right
to left

are you just experiencing

are you keeping a trace in mind
a line
a trajectory

if your hand is
at one place at a time

is there any line
is there any trajectory
you may stop

let your hand come down to a natural
position of rest

you may walk

just be walking

are you keeping a trajectory
in mind

or are you
just at one place at
a time

you may stop

you may place one hand
on your head

is there anything between your hand
and the floor

are you there between your hand
and the floor

where

is there a somewhere

where you are

or just between your hand
and the floor

if this question is senseless

drop it

you may bring your hand down

let it rest naturally

just walk

you may find a place to rest
on the floor

place one hand on your forehead

how far are you willing
to be touched

you may place one hand
on your chest

how far are you willing to be touched

is there anything between your hands
and the floor

if you are between
your hand and the floor

where are you

is there any place
where you are

or are you just there

just resting on the floor

you may slowly stand up

and walk

walk away

away from what

ACKNOWLEDGMENTS

I wish to express my gratitude to people without whom this book would not have been possible, and to people who have supported the project wholeheartedly—first, to Camille Hykes, who has taken a great part in shaping the text into its present form, and then Dean Sluyter, and to the late Maggy Sluyter. I am grateful to Enid Woodward, Evan Zazula, Grad Garside, Peter Davis, and Linda Nockler for organizing workshops in New York; and I am grateful to the students of the Dzogchen Foundation who have attended many of my classes of Gesture of Awareness. I am grateful to my editor at Wisdom Publications, Josh Bartok, whose numerous suggestions helped to clarify the text. And finally, I wish to express my gratitude to my wife Patricia who so encouraged me during the long process of bringing the text forth.

ABOUT THE AUTHOR

Charles Genoud has been a practitioner of Tibetan Buddhism since 1970. He began his studies in Dharamsala, in the School of Dialectics, and was a student of and translator for the Venerable Geshe Rabten for over ten years. While Charles studied and worked with him in Switzerland, Geshe Rabten taught all four schools of Buddhist philosophy, the six perfections, and the *Lamrim Chenmo* of Tsongkhapa. Later, Charles Genoud went on to study closely with Dilgo Khyentse Rinpoche and other teachers in the Dzogchen tradition. He has also practiced Vipassana meditation in Burma and India. Charles Genoud is co-founder of the Vimalakirti Center for Meditation in Geneva, Switzerland. He conducts meditation retreats in the United States, Europe, Brazil, and the Middle East. He is also an assoicate teacher of Lama Surya Das of the Dzogchen Foundation. He lives in Geneva.

ABOUT WISDOM

Wisdom Publications, a nonprofit publisher, is dedicated to making available authentic works relating to Buddhism for the benefit of all. We publish books by ancient and modern masters in all traditions of Buddhism, translations of important texts, and original scholarship. Additionally, we offer books that explore East-West themes unfolding as traditional Buddhism encounters our modern culture in all its aspects. Our titles are published with the appreciation of Buddhism as a living philosophy, and with the special commitment to preserve and transmit important works from Buddhism's many traditions.

To learn more about Wisdom, or to browse books online, visit our website at www.wisdompubs.org.

You may request a copy of our catalog online or by writing to this address:

Wisdom Publications
199 Elm Street
Somerville, Massachusetts 02144 USA
Telephone: 617-776-7416
Fax: 617-776-7841
Email: info@wisdompubs.org
www.wisdompubs.org

THE WISDOM TRUST

As a nonprofit publisher, Wisdom is dedicated to the publication of Dharma books for the benefit of all sentient beings and dependent upon the kindness and generosity of sponsors in order to do so. If you would like to make a donation to Wisdom, you may do so through our website or our Somerville office. If you would like to help sponsor the publication of a book, please write or email us at the address above.

Thank you.

Wisdom is a nonprofit, charitable 501(c)(3) organization affiliated with the Foundation for the Preservation of the Mahayana Tradition (FPMT).